THE INVINCIBLE FAMILY PROJECT

EVERYDAY FAMILIES CREATING HOPE FOR THEIR FUTURE

BOOM POW PUBLISHIN

D1160719

Copyright © 2021 Boom Pow Publishing

Library and Archives Canada Cataloguing in Publications.

Copyright in Ontario Canada & Orlando Florida.

For permissions contact:

hello@marthaekrejci.com

E-Book ISBN: 978-1-990419-04-1

Print ISBN: 978-1-990419-05-8

Hardcover ISBN: 978-1-990419-06-5

1st Edition

Cover by Mike Krejci

CONTENTS

FOREWORD

MARTHA KREJCI

"Perhaps you were created...for such a time as this." - Esther 4:14

We live in a world that is overrun with the idea or narrative that we NEED to work outside the home to be able to provide for the needs inside the home.

That, in my opinion, is degrading us at our very core.

It's tearing our families apart, and leaving our children with the expectations that they don't have much to look forward to.

Our kids don't do what we say, they do what we do.

We can tell them all day long to believe in their dreams and that they can do whatever their little hearts can dream up.

But that isn't what sticks with them.

What we are and what we do sticks with them and allows them to believe that it's what their life will look like too.

That said, I propose we change what they see into what we want to see the world change into.

Crazy, I know! But...it's happening.

With every family I work with, it's happening.

The idea of the family becoming an invincible entity is happening.

They are becoming self-sufficient financially, which leads to freedom in every other aspect you can possibly think of.

Let me leave you with one of my favorite quotes from a woman that saw the vision of this world back in the 1970's. She said this while receiving the Planetary Citizen of the Year award in 1978.

"Never doubt that a small group of thoughtful, committed citizens can change the world; indeed, it's the only thing that ever has." -Margaret Mead

Now, let's do this.

Xo Martha Krejci

MEGGAN'S STORY

I thought that going through cancer when I was twenty-nine years old with two babies at home was going to be the most traumatic thing I'd ever go through. Turns out, what came after was even worse.

I had been trying to make a living from home for the previous five years, but no matter how hard I tried or how much I begged and pleaded, no one wanted to do business with me. I went to business training after business training, implemented all the things, and still failed. The debt was piling up, and we had no savings—not exactly a recipe for success.

We were so broke, in fact, that when I got diagnosed with cancer, I was relieved. I knew God would take care of us through that storm, and for once, I wasn't going to have to worry about money. Five months later, and more chemotherapy, blood transfusions, needle pricks, and naps than I would have ever thought possible, we got through it. I was alive, my babies were okay, my husband had taken care of everything, and we knew who our true friends and family were. Crisis averted, right? Not exactly.

During those five months of cancer, we had absolutely no income. We put everything on credit, and once the cancer was over, we had a giant financial mess. We did our best to stay above water, but after sixteen months of drowning, we had to admit defeat. The calls from creditors were getting aggressive to the point that I was afraid of answering my phone. My hands would shake, and my voice would tremble as I begged and pleaded our case with each and every creditor (there were many). The thing is, they don't care why you got in over your head; they just want their money.

We filed for a consumer proposal, which is essentially bankruptcy, only you pay back a fraction of your debts instead of nothing. I was filled with shame at where we had gotten ourselves. Well-meaning family members reminded us that we should have had savings and told us how irresponsible it was to have been so ill prepared for such a situation. It took years before I could see a new number pop up on my phone and not feel instantly terrified.

A few years later, after we had had our third and final baby (after going through a life-threatening pregnancy), we finally felt like we were doing okay. I still hadn't been able to make a solid income from home, but I was determined to make it work. My husband was back to running his landscaping business full time, and things were looking up.

Then, disaster struck in the form of my parents splitting up after nearly forty years of marriage and needing back the nearly $80,000 loan they had given us. In four months. Suffice it to say, we didn't have the money. Did I also mention that we finished the season with our last client refusing to pay their bill? They felt that my husband did the work too quickly, even though it was done very well, and so we had to take them to court. Once again, we were drowning.

The stress of being so far in debt that any hiccup sends you spiraling is not something I would wish on my worst enemy. Living on practically nothing is worse than all the chemotherapy in the world. I was more afraid about our finances than I ever was about cancer. But still, I refused to give up.

Thirteen years is how long I spent working on myself. I kept hearing that income follows your personal growth, so I just figured I had more growing to do. I was given up for adoption as a baby, so I started my life out feeling rejected. I had a lot of mindset stuff to overcome. I never gave up on the idea of entrepreneurship even though I would have been fully within my right to do so. I believe the desire was planted there by God Himself, and no matter what I did, that desire was never going to be displaced. What I needed was a mentor who had the success I wanted in the way that I wanted it. I couldn't follow another mentor who relied on scripts and cold calls. I needed to learn from someone I aligned with, but sadly, no one was teaching business in a way that felt authentic to me.

Or rather, I hadn't met her yet …

Martha. Freaking. Krejci.

I could have never predicted how much of an impact one human being could have on another before meeting her. I thought I had just found an amazing coach, but what I ended up with was one of my very best friends.

Someone I had been working for sent me a link to Martha's course because she was in the same network marketing company that we were in, and she had reached a rank in six months that typically took three to four years to achieve. That little tidbit caught my attention, but what really sealed the deal for me was that she had done it without hosting a single class.

Excuse me? No classes? No tricking friends and family into coming to a "party" at which I tried to sell something to them? No awkward conversations or having to ask the closing question? There was only one thought in my mind: *Where do I sign up?*

I devoured that $67 course, and it changed everything for me. She talked about ways to get clients to come to me instead of chasing them. She taught me how to lead from my heart and from what I was passionate about. And the best part? She taught me to give everyone an out, no matter what. No more hard selling or anything even closely related to it. It was all so easy breezy with absolutely no pressure. I was, for the first time, showing up authentically as me with no pressure to buy a thing, and can you guess what happened? My business finally began to really take off. After thirteen years of struggle, I had eight people jump into my business the following month without even having to ask for the sale. I was shocked! Could it really be this simple?

I had a blueprint to follow, and for the next couple of months, my business continued to flourish. Unfortunately, I was beginning to see things I didn't like in the people who were in leadership positions within that company. The way that a lot of them were treating Martha was abhorrent. How dare she make money from a course that teaches ***their*** people how to succeed in a way that isn't slimy or gross? You would think that they would have been happy that she was basically doing their job for them, but instead, they were furious. It was like watching the movie *Mean Girls*, and it was disgusting.

When Martha came out with a new course that taught people

how to create multiple streams of high profit income from home, I was first in line. You see, she wasn't just a random lady who had done well in this network marketing company. She was (and had been for some time) a business strategist with a gift of scaling people's businesses in a massive way. That MLM was just *one* of her many income streams of income, and she was actually making over a million dollars per month. Per MONTH! If this wildly successful multi-millionaire was willing to take me under her wing and teach me how to do what she was doing in a way that was authentic and heart-centered and working only five to ten hours a week—who was I to argue?

I made the investment into myself, and then, I went to work. She taught me how to create online courses, how to coach, and most importantly, how to believe in myself. Within a few weeks of starting her course, I had made twenty times my investment. I was able to bring my husband home full-time, we have savings in the bank for the first time in our thirteen-year marriage, and we support our sweet sponsor child, Enock, who developed cerebral malaria and requires hundreds of dollars of medication each month for the next three years. He also needs to be brought to a town several hours away once each quarter to be checked out and restock his medicine. Do you know how amazing it felt to be able to tell the orphanage that we'll cover it for as long as he needs it? Indescribable.

We went from having nothing to being able to effortlessly pay for medication, food, and shelter for another person beyond our immediate family. We are completely debt free, and I haven't had to worry for a long time about whether or not we can afford all the groceries in our cart. I don't hold my breath at the debit machine anymore, praying that the transaction will go through.

I'm on the other side of poverty, and I now know what freedom feels like. Instead of staying stuck in a life that feels like *Groundhog Day*, not able to make ends meet, and terrified that we'll always be in debt, we get to live an extraordinary life. I'm so grateful I never gave up on my dreams. It was worth the wait. And the most beautiful part? This is just the beginning.

ABOUT MEGGAN

Meggan Larson is a best-selling author (The Truth About series), Course Creator, Business Strategist for Martha Krejci, Wife, Mom, and Adoptee. She has a passion for helping women entrepreneurs believe in themselves so fiercely that they become unstoppable forces to be reckoned with.

She has a huge heart for her sponsor child Enock, orphans, broken families, and families who have experienced unexpected financial hardship due to illness. She owns a non-profit called Operation Christmas Spirit which blesses struggling families with gifts and dinner at Christmas in her hometown of Ottawa, Canada where she currently resides with her husband and three children. She loves to laugh at introvert memes, her favourite show is The Office, and she enjoys contemplating the mysteries of the universe by staring up at the night sky. Connect with her at https://megganlarson.com/links

2

LAUREN'S STORY

I never thought that it would happen to me.

Okay, that's inaccurate … and dishonest.

I never thought that I would make those kinds of decisions. The kind that compromises your integrity and betrays the people you love. The kinds of decisions that angry, bitter, and hopeless people make. Not me. Nope.

I had left South Africa with two children under the age of four with a grand total of eight suitcases and one giant dream.

I had walked away from everything and everyone I had ever known in pursuit of a call and vision for the world, for the church, and for my life that was big, bright, and beautiful. I thought that I was unstoppable.

And I really was … for about two years, until it all came crashing down and I lost my way. I buried my dreams; I held a funeral, and I walked away from myself.

And then I met Martha Krejci.

This is my Home-Based Revolution. This is my story.

My husband and I moved our family to Waco, Texas, from our small hometown in South Africa in what can only be described as a mighty move of God (another story for another day). He called us here with a plan and a purpose, and as terrifying as it is to leave everyone and everything we knew, it was clear to us that He was with us and for us, and so we packed up our eight suitcases, sold everything else, and came.

Before the move, I had worked (and loved working) in full time pastoral ministry in our home church, and while it had its challenges (also another story for another day), the path I had mapped out for myself vocationally was a continuation of that journey, my calling.

I would arrive in the US to work at a non-profit for a year and then transition into the dual-master's degree program that I was invited to apply for just two years prior, the program that literally started this entire adventure in the first place. From there, the world would be my oyster. I would start my own consultancy company, where I would bring my passion for wisdom and the accessibility of peace and flourishing for all areas of our lives, combine it with my social work training, and turn it into service of the church (my first love). I would write books, speak on stages, and start a non-profit which would reach back into my home country and create access to some of the resources and opportunities that I have here.

Easy peasy lemon squeezy.

Or so I thought.

As we rolled into year two of our adventure, the adrenaline rush started to wear off, and what can only be described as a wave of grief crashed over and into me, leaving me all but completely paralyzed. I entered into a very dark place.

That same year, I got into a car wreck, which injured my neck and signed me up for eight months of intense physical therapy (two hours a day, three days a week). Just two months after that, my three-year-old son fell six feet and snapped his jaw on both sides of his face. The aftermath of those accidents, together with that tidal wave of grief that was already suffocating me, woke up some old PTSD that had been asleep beneath the surface of my life for nearly a decade. I deferred the start of my grad school program by a semester. I deferred my dreams, and then, I completely unravelled.

I wish I could say it was one of those poetic unravellings where you lose everything and then find everything and it's pretty and neat at the end, but that would be a lie. It was ugly and scary. I was ugly and scary.

I was mean, impatient, explosive, and guarded. I withdrew further and further into my cave and further and further into the darkness. I began to forget who I was and who my God was. I shut out and ignored the beautiful love and supportive community that I had and turned my heart towards the whispers and false promises of attention that, had I not come to my senses, would have completely destroyed my family and all of our lives.

But I did come to my senses, and just as I began to claw my way back to the life I thought I had left home and country for, I fell pregnant. After Ellie was born, more than half of our savings went to paying hospital bills, and the other half went to immigration bills. I decided to come to terms with the fact that my life was just not going to turn out how I had planned. After one whole semester at grad school, I dropped out. My golden ticket, the first and most important step toward my calling: cancelled.

I could see no other path forward.

In the remaining cloud of darkness that enveloped me, I could see no alternate routes.

It was over.

RIP dreams, RIP calling. I'll be over here, settling for my consolation prize.

Enter Martha Krejci.

Honestly, I was only in it for the money.

I needed to work because I am not cut out for stay-at-home motherhood. It's just not for me. That being said, I was starting to realize that employment here in the U.S. isn't exactly family-friendly, and I didn't have the patience or the grace to deal with that, so I chose self-employment.

If I wasn't going to live my dreams or get to live and breathe and move in the sweet spot of God's call on my life, then I would at least get rich and use whatever gifts and talents I had to do it.

If a dual-master's degree was a golden ticket to my dreams, the Home-Based Revolution was supposed to be the golden ticket to my consolation prize, to wherever it was that I would settle and live a comfortable life where I could at least choose my own hours and feel just a little bit useful.

Oh boy, was I in for a surprise! I signed up for a business strategy mentor and coaching and ended up with:

- A real, healthy, and loving community and friends for life.
- Business strategy and mentorship that is so heart-

centered and healing that it woke up the parts of me that I thought were dead and buried.

- Healing. Oh, my gosh. The darkness that had enveloped and was suffocating me has dissipated; the festering wounds that caused it are healing.

My dreams have been resurrected; they are brighter and clearer than ever. More importantly, I also have the tools to turn them into reality.

The work I have done in HBR has helped me realize that God can use any path and that I don't need a graduate degree to make a difference.

My business uses my experience in social work and ministry to inspire and empower women to get back into the driver's seat of their own lives, to reimagine and rewrite the scripts that are holding them and their callings captive. I am still in ministry; it just looks a little different than I thought it would three years ago.

I've written a book and have been a part of three others, with at least another four on the horizon.

I am also just about ready to launch that non-profit.

My transformation is actually at my very core. I see God, myself, my world with more clarity than I ever have.

My dreams, the hope I have for the future, my belief that I have a responsibility to steward them and to turn them into reality ... all of that is a natural outcome and downstream consequence of the real story, which is that I had all but forgotten who I was, who my God was, and what He had called me to do. Now, I remember.

I thought I was signing up for a course that would give me permission and the means to settle. To settle for a life lived around making enough money and making enough of a contribution to be able to say I do 'something.' An added bonus would be that, in doing so, I could numb the pain of the loss and disappointment of the past three years.

What I got instead was a returning to it, digging up what I had buried to find it just barely breathing, and having the courage to breathe new life into it.

Flesh and blood and sinew on a graveyard of dry bones.

That is my HBR transformation.

ABOUT LAUREN

Lauren da Silva has two great loves: human beings & learning, and so she is always finding ways to channel her loves into her passion: Making true human flourishing as accessible to as many people as possible.

As a recovering people-pleaser and co-dependent, she knows first hand how dangerous and limiting it can be to sit in the backseat of your own life while allowing other people, the status quo or even the culture around you to take the wheel of your life and life's mission.

That is why she is on a mission to inspire and equip as many women as possible to not just flip the script they're living (or feeling trapped) in, but to re-imagine and re-write it completely.

She is all about helping women just like her give up trading their authenticity for love and belonging, and instead trade their shame and judgement for curiosity, their fear for courage and their isolation for true belonging.

When she is not reading, writing, teaching or coaching, you can find her painting, wandering around in the woods, or in her backyard tending to her butterfly garden with her children and her small flock of backyard chickens :)

Connect with Lauren at https://laurendasilva.org/links

3

CINDY'S STORY

As worship started that Sunday morning, I went to social media to share the service. As I did, I saw a new message on my phone. Thinking it was our daughter, I clicked over and checked it out. To my surprise, it was a message from someone I had spoken with a couple of days before about her system for creating a successful home business. The message stated that she was running a flash sale on her course and wanted me to know in case I was ready to jump in.

I turned the phone to my husband. He looked at me and said, "You know where the money is." This started the first of many crying episodes for me. You see, I had prayed before falling asleep the night before that she would offer this to me at a discount if it was meant to be.

Now, let me go back about fifteen years. At the time, I was a homeschooling mom of one child, and she was about to finish high school. I knew it was time to do more as I saw that season ending for me. I started looking for a job. For four months, I sent out resumes, made calls, and did everything you were supposed to do, but no one would hire me. When I could get a hiring manager to look at my resume, they would play down my life skills. I was told repeatedly that the previous eighteen years of my life were not relevant in the job market.

I finally landed a low paying, customer service job in a large telecom. It was a contract ninety-day position that I looked at as getting paid to go back to school. I had to tell myself something to make sense of the reality that after gas and other expenses, I would be bringing home almost nothing.

That ninety-day position turned into ten years with that company. I learned so much and grew as a person. And the more I learned, the more my confidence grew. I did unimaginable things for someone who came into the company with, according to hiring managers, no marketable skills. Within six months, I was in a leadership position as a team lead. A few months later, I was put into an interim supervisor role but failed miserably due to not understanding that managing is not leading. I stepped down from that position and moved to the corporate side of the company. In my years there, I was given so many opportunities. This is when I was able to finally draw on my life skills.

I planned, coordinated, and led events all over the country for senior VPs all the way up to the CEO of the company. I worked with many of the top executives, which allowed me to learn from them directly. Watching how they managed their departments and led their people was invaluable. I also worked in back office systems and learned how to set up trainings and implement them. And I handled a million-dollar state grant and brought it to conclusion, spending the million dollars given to us to within a few thousand dollars of the allotted amount.

Yes, my confidence soared, but things weren't all I wanted them to be. There was a job I wanted to do, training facilitator, but I was told, "You can't." The reason? I didn't have a college degree. It didn't matter that I could do the work, I wasn't qualified, according to their set standards. This is where my story takes a turn.

The "you can't" statements didn't hold me back. I was determined to do what I knew I could do, despite what I was told. And I was determined to do it without a degree.

Through those years at the corporate office, I started working on myself. I found a network marketing company I liked and thought I would build a business through them. Though I was not successful, I found the world of personal development and dove head first into it. I found entrepreneurship and realized my soul was burning to enter that world. As I worked on myself, my love of writing started to re-emerge in my life. So, after ten years with the company, I took a voluntary layoff and came home to start my own business. I planned to blog my way into success. Others had done it, and I firmly believed that if they could, I could too.

Though I followed all the rules, I failed, and back into the workforce I went. This is where things took another turn. Remember how I stated I had failed miserably at leadership before? Well, I stepped back into a leadership role, this time knowing how to lead. I had learned this from all the personal development I had been doing.

The company I went to work for was one of the most hated companies in our area, and they needed their customer service turned around. When I left two years later, the customer service department was unrecognizable from what it had been when I arrived. I am not bragging, simply stating facts. I worked hard and led a team that worked hard. It was not a one person show. True leadership never is.

This time, when I came back home, I started a small stop gap business to allow me to stay home. I was determined to have my own business and knew all I needed were the right tools. I had tried so many programs from so many gurus, though, I was beginning to wonder if the right tools existed.

Back to the worship service and the message I had received ... Enter Martha Krejci!

And enter my life she did. She brought not only the right tools into my life but also the whole tool kit! At the time of my writing this, that Sunday was ten months ago. Since then, using her tool kit, I started a following on social media that grew so quickly I had to get help to handle it. Recently, I became a best-selling author, fulfilling a life-long dream. I have also created and launched a course helping women save ten to fifteen years in finding their life purpose and learning to walk in it, no matter the season of life they are in. Creating and facilitating this course and the mentoring surrounding it have completely canceled that "you can't" from a few years back. I also stepped back into the world of direct sales, creating another stream of income that is taking off with rocket boosters. All of this I learned from Martha's toolkit, HBR – Home-Based Revolution!

As good as all of that is and though it is the direction I wanted for my life, the most important changes due to finding Martha and using her tool kit are listed below:

- A heart for service.
- The knowledge that confidence is good, but you need the right tools to be successful.
- Realizing success is wonderful, but love and caring are better.

- A belief that not everyone out there is simply trying to sell you something. Some want to see you succeed.
- A community of like-minded women who cheer you on when you succeed and lift you up when you fall.

Martha calls me sassy because of my confidence. Maybe you are like me, sassy with all the confidence you need, but you still have not uncovered success. First, I want you to know my confidence comes from God, the gifts He has given me, and the promises He has made to me. Second, I want you to know that all the confidence in the world will not get you far without the right tools, without a good tool kit. It's like trying to drive the most awesome car in the world with no fuel. HBR will provide the fuel for your confidence and guide you in how to take your passions to the next level and monetize them.

Ready ... Set ... Let's Go!

ABOUT CINDY

Cindy sees her main role in life as an encourager. She has been a mentor to teens and adults for over 30 years.

After being a stay at home, home schooling mom for 18 years, she re-entered the workforce in 2007, working for a major telecom. This company afforded her many opportunities to wear many different hats. Within six months of joining the company she received a promotion to a leadership role. Then, 2 years later she discovered personal development and her life changed completely. About that same time, she left the leadership role to take a position in the HR Training and Leadership department within the same company. During her years in that department and working for and with some of the top executives in this company she learned leadership firsthand. Managing projects and leading people within those projects taught her skills necessary for leadership and coaching.

In 2016 Cindy took a voluntary separation from the telecom and worked from home writing and learning more in the field of personal development.

Wanting to return to the leadership arena, Cindy went back into the workforce as a customer service manager. Her time was spent grooming and leading a team that could turn the customer service experience around for their company. This time allowed her to apply what she had learned and see for herself what does and does not work. She had learned in her past experiences, you cannot manage people and if you try, your turnover rate will be high. You must lead the people and manage the work. Using this philosophy allowed her to build a strong team.

In 2019, Cindy separated from this company and came home to start her own business. She started a successful small book-keeping service as a stop gap until she could move into the field of her calling, personal development.

She is a bestselling published author, a professional speaker, a mentor, and a business strategist for Martha Krejci.

Cindy is married to Michael and together they have one child, Sarah. She is active in her church and sees every aspect of her life as her ministry.

Connect with her at https://cindydement.com/links

4

SHANNON'S STORY

I had my second midlife crisis at thirty-five. It was Memorial Day, 2019. I had just come home from a weekend trip to visit my grandparents, and I was lost. Sometime on the three-hour drive home, I began to feel the need to escape. I had felt that way once before, but that was when I was eighteen. I didn't understand why I felt this way. I had purposely rebuilt my world, so I wouldn't feel that way again. My life was great. I had a house, a loving boyfriend, a great circle of friends, and I was being considered for my dream job. Everything was great. What the H-E-Double Hockey Sticks was going on?

Apparently, things were not great. Of course, I didn't realize this until a couple hours later, after an epic fight with my significant other. You know, the one where you end an eight-year relationship because he won't hug you. Yup. That was my breaking point. Me, emotionally distraught over something trivial, finally nuking what had been a crumbling relationship for years, all because he wouldn't hold me while I cried.

Now, looking back almost three years later, I realize that was a bit unfair. We were not a touchy-feely couple. We didn't lean on each other for support. We didn't deal with emotions, and I sure as heck didn't cry, especially full-bodied drooly tears while babbling and screaming incoherently in a pillow. So I can see how he may have been unprepared for that, and I may not have shown the understanding he required in that moment. Going nuclear, as my friends call my past-the-point-of-reason temper, was not the mature thing to do that day, but I realize now that it was the decision that saved my life.

As I sat in my bedroom, watching him transfer his personal items to the guest room of the house we had built together two years before, I began to accept that I hated my life. Was I depressed? Doubtful. Did I want to kill myself? Absolutely not. Did I dislike everything about myself and the decisions I had made? Wholeheartedly. I wanted to just crawl out of my skin and start fresh. Now, for some people, the go getting "I see rainbows" people of the world, starting over sounds fantastic. For me, a disabled thirty-something chick who just broke up with the only boy who ever loved her? Not so much. I felt like I'd just been abandoned at Mount Everest base camp with no rope or parka.

So I ran away. Not literally, of course. I have cerebral palsy and am one of the lucky ones that can walk. But, no, running has never been an option. Nor driving, skateboarding, or riding a bike—but that's a chapter for another book. For the first time in my life, I ran from my problems and, quite frankly, ignored them. I spent that summer figuring out who I was, while trying to spend as little time as possible at home with my ex boyfriend/now roommate.

It was the oddest but best summer of my life. Probably top five in my entire existence. It was the summer that I found myself again. I discovered that, somehow, during the duration of my relationship with my ex, I had lost myself. The vibrant, energetic, extroverted, potty-mouthed girl who rocked the first half of her twenties was gone. In her place was this disappointing and deflated version of me.

As I let myself get dragged about the west coast, road tripping to a convention for my bestie's MLM and failing miserably at any sort of flirtatious communication with the male species, I remembered what fun was like. I volunteered with a non-profit I loved, re-learned how to do things impulsively, and became aware of how apologetic I was about everything. It was ridiculous. Embarrassingly ridiculous. Slowly, the fog went away. I could see the results of my choices over the last couple years, and I began to question just how "emotionally healthy" I was. Needless to say, I wasn't liking the conclusions I was coming to.

I was a scrambled egg stuck inside a pristine shell. I looked fine, but inside, I was a wreck. A messy, goopy, *$%*!@$ wreck. The worst part of it all, I didn't even believe in myself. Like, when did this happen? I had no clue. I totally felt alien in my "single" body. There I was, sitting in a booth, sharing pizza with an attractive man who thought I was gorgeous, funny, and brilliant. The nicer he was to me, the more I questioned his motives and intelligence, unknowingly sabotaging the fragile bond we were starting to build. Yeah, I was becoming a stage five clinger.

Luckily, though, I had a moment of courage and started to communicate. I began talking to my friends and sharing what the last several years had been like. I apologized a lot—but this time for the friendship crimes I was guilty of, not for my general existence. I went deep and told that amazing man all about the nonsense my insecurities were generating in my head. And guess what? This one didn't run away; he actually stayed around for a bit.

Somehow, as fall turned into winter, I decided that the nuke

I'd dropped on my life months before hadn't destroyed everything; it had simply reformatted it. I was less glitchy. I was moving forward. I had finally stopped being scared and began taking my life back. I was adulting, and I was slowly going broke.

Adulting is expensive, or, at least, my version of it is. And I was in a selfish phase where I wasn't willing to give up ANY of the things I enjoyed. I needed a job. To be fair, I'm still in that selfish phase, so maybe this isn't a phase; it really could just be who I am now. Anyway, like most people, I needed more money. Of course, my bestie had a solution—work the business side of that MLM convention we went to. "It'll change your life. You'll make your dreams come true."

Uh huh. Yeah, if you're into endless rejection, live for being the super annoying "Have you tried this?" friend, and find great pleasure in having casual strangers zone out during your presentations while eating all your good snacks. I. Am. Not. That. Girl. But ... I didn't want a nine to five job again. Frankly, it was more hassle than it was worth thanks to my disability. Arranging for rides, resentful bosses that continually upped their expectations, and, of course, the phones. I had just stopped having dreams about taking call center orders. I was healing. There was no way I was ever going back to that.

But I needed something. I wanted something I could do at home, where I could make my own hours and not worry about coordinating my work schedule with someone else's ability to give me a lift. So I did what any good sensible go-getter would do. I bought a program, a multiple income stream course and coaching program. I networked myself into a group of amazing women who were supportive and looking for empowerment and financial freedom just like me. And I did absolutely nothing with it.

It's been a year since I bought the program. A year since I could've been dancing in more money than I could ever dream of. A year since I could've launched an income stream or two that would have changed my life and made all my dreams come true. I didn't do any of these things because I wasn't ready. I needed to heal.

In the year and a half since I've met my mentor, Martha Krejci, I haven't made a dime. It's not because her process doesn't work; I know it does. I've watched it work for others countless times. I haven't made money because I wasn't in a place where I could make it work. As I mentioned earlier, I was a mess. Scrambled eggs. Instead of focusing on how to use her tools to provide additional income for my new life, I used her resources and tools to fix myself.

I focused on me. I made myself emotionally and mentally healthy again. I put the puzzle back together and came out transformed, full of energy, confidence, and trust — three things I was seriously lacking when I met her. I allowed love. From myself and others. I even fell in love with that amazing man I had pizza with, who I knew was insane for thinking I was great. And when he asked me to marry him, I said yes.

Two years ago, I thought my life was over. I thought I was going to be alone, regretting my impulsive decision to break it off for the rest of my life. Now, I'm married to the person who is just right for me. I have a job I love that doesn't feel like work, and I get to help people who have been where I was figure their lives out and move into the future they want. I can honestly say, I don't know the girl I was two years ago before I began my self-discovery, but I absolutely adore the woman I have become because of the risk I took investing in myself. Thank you, Martha, for teaching me how to believe in myself. It took almost forty years, but I finally do appreciate who I am.

ABOUT SHANNON

Shannon Cochron is an advocate, personal development coach, entreprenuer. She also moonlights as a clerk for Grants Pass Downs. A wife and lifelong sports enthusiast, she teaches physically impaired individuals how to adjust their lives around their physical limitations and find financial freedom. Born with a disability herself, she's passionate about helping others with physical challenges create a meaningful life for themselves and understands the limitations the current system provides. After watching her husband struggle after a life altering injury, she began working to help bridge the gap for the newly disabled.

If you're interested in learning more, check out her website https://www.shannoncochron.com/discover to access her free resources and and discover a community that's becoming handicapable.

5

LYDIA'S STORY

Summer of 2019 was the ugliest and hardest summer I ever lived through. That Lydia was a really angry and out-of-control stay-at-home mom. She spoke hurtfully and spitefully to her children—and found a grim satisfaction in making them feel sad and scared. I feel appalled and devastated even as I type this because no one knew. I was just that broken and wanted my family to feel the hurt and the despair I felt. Yet, it didn't make it any better, only worse.

This Lydia would start each day lying in bed, eyes closed, contemplating how she could just end her life. The voices in her head were saying that no one would miss her when she was gone, that her family would be better off without her. It was a really tough place. What I didn't realize was that my anger and extreme sadness were because I was living a double life.

I had latched onto this idea that if I could somehow be a teacher turned persuasive sales person, I would make tens of thousands of dollars a month. What I didn't account for was the amount of hours away from home and energy drain and people-pleasing it would take. With every class and party event, I felt like a straight up dancing bear. And I was getting sick of it. Nevertheless, I was convinced that unless I put on an extrovert go-getter mask to show up, no one would support me. Pair that with a healthy FOWOPT (fear of what other people think), and you've got a cocktail for fast burnout and high resentment. In reality, I was sacrificing myself - my very soul - for *money*. Sounds pretty stupid, huh? But that's literally where I was. I was convinced that I had no value unless I was making money.

Looking back, I now recognize what was happening; my façade and my true purpose were clashing heads. But the victory would come - and in an unexpected way.

God has a unique way of answering my prayers. In this case, my goal was to find out how my work friends were rocking their business. I wondered aloud, "What is it that _____ uses to grow her business effortlessly?" No more than two or three days later, this same person invited me into her leadership training group to share about prospecting analytical introverts (like me). It was there that I was inadvertently introduced to a new group on Facebook called Goldgetters. "That must be her secret strategy," I thought. A few clicks later, I found myself in this brand new training group—and on a slow upward but powerful track towards The Martha Krejci.

Oh, my word. Let me tell you about this Martha.

She was a woman who grew her business in record time to a top rank and – get this - without teaching a single class (ex-squeeze me?!). Martha grew her business authentically and completely her way. This Midwestern chick with straight So Cal vibes always shared from the heart. She was goofy and passionate and just real. She was my kinda people, someone I could easily hang out with and talk '90s sitcoms for hours and not feel weird. She *got* me.

So when Martha said, "Here are some resources that you can use. And oh, by the way, I created a quick course that you can use. Check it out," I jumped in. And I gotta be honest—at first, I was *not* impressed! I thought, "Wait, hold on. I think I must be missing it. This system is working for her?! No! It cannot be this stinkin' *simple*." I eventually got over my initial shock (and relative level of cynicism) when I saw the testimonials. This defied logic to me – less time and energy, yet exponential return!? The method didn't make sense, but clearly, the results spoke for themselves. So I tried things Martha's way ... and I actually had success! When her next course came out, I immediately picked it up. And so the cycle began where the next thing she would put out, I was in. Daily prompts? Sign me up! Finding business builders? I'm there! Wash, rinse, repeat.

Before I knew it, I was looking at a screen, signing up for Home-Based Revolution.

I distinctly remember my conversation with Martha. When she told me what it would cost and the kind of impact it would have on my life and my family, I was in shock. And it wasn't sticker shock the way you think—I was shocked at how *inexpensive* it was! This was immense value for a very affordable cost. I remember literally shaking and being on the verge of tears when I saw her invitation to HBR. I told my husband, *"I can't not sign up for this*! I tried the other way, attempting to be what other people wanted me to be, and failed. I am tired of growing other people's businesses and seeing no return."* This was a golden opportunity for me to learn directly from Martha how to grow a business authentically. Hell yeah, I'm in! So I signed up. And then, the roller coaster ride started.

Remember when I talked about selling out my soul for the idea of five figures? I was ready to do it again but with someone I trusted. And God knew Martha was who I needed. There was a process that I needed to go through—and it had nothing to do with money.

Hear me when I say this: Martha is trustworthy. Her heart is truly for her people.

She said to me, "Yes, there's money—there's money waiting for you in abundance.

"Don't even worry about that. Set that off to the side in your mind.

"What I need for you to do is to reclaim your soul.

"I need you to reclaim your heart. I need you to reclaim your story.

"I need for you to see the places that you have toiled, that you were hurt. The places where you didn't think there was a light at the end of the tunnel, and yet, you found it.

"*That* is what you need to share with your people.

"You need to let them know that they're not alone.

"You need to let them know that there's a way out.

"And because you know how valuable it was to you to find a way out, it will be of same, if not greater, value to them."

So that's what I did. I looked at my story to find those places where I experienced "overnight success" that was years in the making. As it turns out, my gift has literally been with me my entire life. In HBR, I found permission to open the door to my true self again. I also found lifelong friends who see and fiercely fight for my genius—and I for them.

Now, I am no longer that angry, depressed mom or the "dancing bear" who gets used by others to meet their agenda. They meant no malice; I was a willing participant. Thinking back, that's the part that hits the hardest. I was a willing participant because I didn't value myself. With God's help, Martha changed all that.

Now I have a renewed mission: to help women who were

like me—frazzled and unfulfilled yet ready for more. I help them take the brave step to walk away from other people's expectations so they can rediscover the path that they were *born* to walk on. There's literally no other feeling like the flowing of your own genius—your God-given, divine timing appointed, light shining genius. And what I love even more is my gift of helping people discover their genius allows me to do the same with my kids, my husband, and my friends. Each "genius gem" is truly a miracle!

My invitation to you is to choose to value your soul and your story. Discover your genius and let it sing out in all you do. And if you accept the invitation, your life's greatest adventure awaits —with awesome community and transformation along the way! It's all worth it.

ABOUT LYDIA

Lydia is an entrepreneur, vision catalyst, and public speaker. She is also a grateful wife, mom, and avid rock climber.

Her life mission is empowering women to live fully alive from their unique purpose. She helps them rediscover their WHY hidden in their personal stories, reclaim their identity, and live confidently in their genius.

After six years as an engineer turned reluctant stay-at-home mom, she discovered her unique voice for a generation feeling torn between career and motherhood. She found the key to experiencing the best of both worlds and is on a mission to help other women find their brand of joy, peace, and fulfillment.

If you are ready to rediscover your purpose, shine in your genius, live a thriving life, and serve your world from the heart, connect with Lydia and grab the resources you need to embark on your greatest adventure!

Connect with her at https://lydiaeppic.com/links

6

TARA'S STORY

When I first started homeschooling, I was scared I would screw up my kids. I had no degree in education. No one in my family had ever done this. Some relatives had expressed their concerns for the kids' futures and well-being. Our mad experiment to raise our children up in a faith-based home education would only show its results in time. By then, it would probably be too late. The damage would be done, the naysayers proven right, and I would stand guilty as charged.

Despite all these doubts and fears, I held on to the hope that God was bigger than my frailty and many inadequacies. He had blessed us with four amazing children so far and the grace to trust Him with our family size. He had provided grace for us to welcome these children and those yet to come. I knew we would be misunderstood as Christians by many well-meaning people in our lives. Even sometimes by fellow Christians. Home-schooling was just another crazy thing on our pile of crazy. So when our first-born daughter was five years old, I ripped off the

Band-Aid of fear and started figuring out how to homeschool from scratch.

We kept it simple by focusing on the '3R's' (reading, 'riting and 'rithmetic). I plugged into our local homeschool group for what it was worth and slowly began to figure this out. Soon, her twin brothers joined the fray, and I was homeschooling in earnest with five kids under six and another one on the way.

Ten years later, I was juggling a full household of ten kids, seven of which were active homeschoolers. The naysayers had been silenced by the results shown in our older kids. They were all bright, well spoken, capable young people with individual interests, pursuits, and personalities (even the twins!). I was feeling pretty accomplished about myself as a homeschool mom. I had developed a reputation for being a kind of "super mom" as a mom of many, so a lot of people came to me for advice on everything big family and homeschool related.

Then, four blows came in one year that almost threw me to the ground. Our ninth born was not speaking properly by eighteen months, so it came as no surprise when she was diagnosed as significantly speech delayed. Doing virtual speech therapy was new and intimidating, yet what choice did I have but to go forward into the unknown and help her? While this was happening, our fourth born began testing for Asperger's. I had long suspected that his highly introverted tendencies and intense focus were different. I knew nothing about autism or Asperger's. Again, into the unknown I went, holding tight to God's hand to keep me steady. Shortly after, our tenth born was diagnosed as severely speech delayed. *Severely*. I didn't want to tell anyone. It felt like a report card was coming in telling me that I was failing miserably as a home educator and mother. Three children with learning-related issues in less than a year? I was scared to tell my parents and in-laws, expecting them to say,

"We tried to warn you." I didn't even want to tell my dear sister yet. Only my husband knew.

Then, the final blow came, and I lost my footing. Our sixth born son had been struggling to learn since we started his formal homeschool lessons at age six just like all the other kids before him. They had all learned how to read, write, and do basic math with no problem using the same resources and approach. He was different. Two years into his home education, something was clearly wrong. Despite having a two-year head start, his six-year-old brother was quickly overtaking him in learning to read. I was scared to know the truth yet more scared not to. We got him assessed by a professional and waited a week for the results.

In that same season of life, I had just started a business training program called The Home-Based Revolution. The plan was to follow Martha Krejci's proven system of creating 10K a month in only five to ten hours a week of working from home doing something uniquely authentic to who I am and in service to others. My sister had done it successfully in less than a year, so I was in. As a big family, we had long ago given up on our dreams of doing anything beyond just making ends meet. I hardly dared to dream that I could help create a profitable business from home on only five to ten hours a week doing something I loved. As I started the HBR training, I complimented it with the highly recommended 'Big Think' mini course to deal with obstacles holding me back. I found time in my full days and finished it the very night before the news came.

I knew he was delayed. Hearing just how delayed almost broke me. "Your son is presenting below the first percentile in reading, writing, and math." *Below the first percentile.* My heart broke for him. For me. Every fear, self-doubt, and accusation about me as a homeschool mom came screaming back to me that day. Who was I kidding? Four kids in one year with learning-related issues. Did I need any more proof of my total lack as a homeschool mother? That having a big family was a sure plan to screw kids up? I felt sick with guilt and fear. I went through the day in a fog, just going through the motions of caring for my family until I could be alone.

That night, I got alone with God to lay out my heartbreak and fears. I expected comfort. I didn't expect what happened next.

Everything I learned in "The Big Think" started coming back to me in a whole new light. I thought I would apply those strategies to business. Not my family. Not homeschooling. Not my assumed abysmal failure as a homeschool mother.

Louder than my feelings and fears came one message from The Big Think: "I'm just a few steps ahead of another mom who will go through the same thing." I began to see my situation in a whole new light. God had brought me to this that I might go through this and, in turn, be the hand reaching back to someone else in the future. Could it be? Was it possible that I was not an utter failure as a homeschool mom? Was it possible that their challenges were not my fault but, instead, a mystery of God's plan and purpose in and through our lives as a family? Hope began to kindle in my heart. Truth that I was His and He is mine washed over me, melting away my fears. I began to weep in gratitude because I saw that He had prepared me to be knocked down so that I might find His grace to get back up again.

The little spark of hope kept growing brighter. I felt courage rising and a fierce maternal love that only moms understand. With a flame of courage and hope blazing inside me, I 'picked up my mat and walked.' The pity party was over. I wiped my eyes, took a deep breath, and told my husband the news. The next day, I pushed through a barrier of fear by sharing all this with Martha and the amazing HBR women in a group coaching call.

I am so grateful to God for His perfect timing. I know more clearly than ever that He has chosen me to be the mom to these exact children for such a time as this. He orchestrated circumstances in such a perfect way for me to have exactly what I needed in the hour I would need it. He helped me see things in a new way by connecting me with just the right people at just the right time. Rather than be knocked down and give up on our dreams, goals, and values, I am rising up as a woman, wife, and homeschool mom of many. Rather than 'screwing them up,' I am raising them up in God's grace and truth. I will support, bless, and prepare all my children for the future God has planned for them, and I will learn what I need to do so. I can do all things through Christ who strengthens me.

The road that has led me here has meaning and purpose beyond anything I could have asked or imagined. A few years from now, when another homeschooling mom is in that same place of doubt, pain, and fear, I will be the hand reaching out in the dark saying, "It's okay. I've been there. I will help you." Together, by God's grace, we will rise above our circumstances to bless our families and communities with courage, love, and hope born in the fire of tribulation. The challenges I am overcoming today will be the hope for others tomorrow, beginning at home, then going out into our circles, communities, and the world.

ABOUT TARA

Tara Lee Hills is a Christian, wife and homeschool mom of ten children (with another blessing on the way!). She has been featured in Dr.Phil, The Washington Post, ABC News, CBC Marketplace & Global News among other places. In her spare time she writes books, creates courses and helps other big family moms overcome struggles and grow in grace.

When people ask her how she does it all she smiles remembering that she hadn't changed a diaper when she first became a mom. She loves to share her journey from unprepared and controlling to confident and trusting to encourage and equip other moms with 3 or more children.

She now lives outside Ottawa in Canada where she homeschools full time, works part time alongside her husband in their multiple home businesses, and grows in God's grace day by day.

She can be found at https://taraleehills.com/links. Feel free to connect with her, grab her free resources, join her online community and grow in grace with her!

7

TERESA'S STORY

My story starts in 2010 when I crashed and burned in nursing and fell into major depression. My husband and I had owned a hospice agency and served hundreds of patients and families over the years. While I had always had compassion for those with mental illness, I never believed it would happen to me. But it did, and I couldn't work for three years.

During that time, we lost everything. We sold our hospice, which had been worth millions, for pennies. Our aging care homes closed. We let our home go back to the bank, and we went to live in a fixer-upper farmhouse we had bought with cash years before. The house wasn't ready to be lived in, but it's where we landed. There was even a period of time when I didn't know if I would ever be able to work as a nurse again, and I considered applying for disability.

Left with more than $900,000 in debt, Greg and I started anew. We somehow lived on $400/week while I was recovering because I wasn't well enough to be left alone. This kept Greg from working a full-time job but meant I would be safe.

As I rested at home to recover, I had new stressors of not knowing who I was outside of being a nurse. The painful reality was that my entire identity was wrapped up in me being a nurse. Without that, I didn't know who I was or how I even mattered in the world. The three years I spent in recovery were both the best and worst of my life, and I wouldn't trade them for anything because I learned how to care for myself, and I learned my value as a person.

While keeping me safe and helping with my recovery, Greg whittled down our debt by selling any properties we owned and anything we didn't need. I returned to work as a nurse in 2014 and had several really good years. We were officially debt free in 2017, and things were looking up!

Then, in August 2020, I had my first real flare up of major depression. And one day, I literally had to pick up the phone in tears to quit my job immediately. I gave no notice and was truly an emotional wreck.

What scared me the most was that the anxiety, depression, and tearfulness I was experiencing was as severe as what had happened ten years earlier. My biggest fear was losing another three years to recover. We were finally beginning to rebuild our lives, and I was back at square one.

Here I sat, once again, at home recovering from depression and with the stress of being without 60% of our income. Ever the entrepreneur, I couldn't just sit on the couch and rest. I began exploring what might be next for me. I began to reach back to my entrepreneurial roots and stumbled onto Martha Krejci and her course, The Home-Based Revolution.

I had no idea how we would afford it since I wasn't working. I asked my husband about it, and he said what I already knew. We just didn't have the money. One Sunday, we prayed about it. Immediately after we offered that prayer, I received a message from Martha saying I could get into HBR for 50% off. This was a God thing, for sure, and Greg and I immediately agreed to purchase the course and move forward.

One of the best ways for me to manage depression is to add structure to my days. I began to consume the course content on a regular schedule and participate in all the coaching calls. I was learning a new language, one filled with love, positivity, and hope. I felt nurtured and able to dream again.

While I knew how to grow a brick-and-mortar business with feet on the ground and grassroots marketing, growing a business in the digital space had eluded me. I had spent thousands of dollars on workshops and training courses that promised me I would be successful. One launch and one failure at a time, I conditioned myself to believe that an online business would probably never work for me.

I started doing the course work, which, in the beginning, was all about working on me. I stared my limiting beliefs in the face and learned how to see them for what they were: old limiting beliefs. I started working on courses and defining who I wanted to serve. I began to grow a community, and I found that others valued my message.

For the first time in my life, I was able to launch courses online with sales. It felt so good to be able to contribute to our household income in a different way. And as I forged a new direction in my life, my depressive symptoms were again easily managed. Better yet, I was able to release past failures and emotions that had kept me from success for ten years.

One day, as I was thinking through my life's journey and all that had happened with the hospice from the growth to the loss, I was able to clearly see the gold that I had left behind from that experience. I had grown a hospice to $3 million with just a $6,000 investment.

There was so much joy in that growth and experience that was intended for me. Our hospice had been dedicated to God in service of His precious ones. He had blessed my efforts by removing barriers to my messages and giving me the wisdom to speak the right words to the right people at the right time. He had blessed the hospice with phenomenal growth.

And then, He took it away. I personally believe my experience with depression was intended for me. I believe God knew I was tired and was not going to remove myself from my work, so He did it for me.

I can now see what was left behind was a great gift of how I can help others take care of His precious ones. It is not my place anymore to serve at the bedside of the dying but, instead, to help those who are in that place to serve as many as they can. By serving in this way, I can take care of myself and still serve a population that I so treasure.

My future is so bright, and I have no doubt that my abundance is coming to me. Through HBR, I have reclaimed my power, released my losses, and moved through things that years of talk therapy could not help me get beyond.

I'm now on a mission to help nurse entrepreneurs and hospices get in front of medical and community referral sources, so they can serve more patients. I am helping nurses back away from burnout with free nursing continuing education for life on my website, www.TheNursingConnection.com. And I am leading and serving from the heart.

I was blessed to have some time to chat with Martha Krejci about my story and my business. She looked me straight in the eye and said some words I will never forget.

"You need to take your seat at the table."

I am forever grateful.

ABOUT TERESA

Teresa is a fun-loving, homesteader and RN who launched her own hospice and grew it to $3M with just a $6K investment! She is a wife, mother of 5, and is known as Grammy to the littlest in the family.

Teresa helps nurse entrepreneurs and hospices get in front of medical and community referral sources so they can serve more patients and grow their businesses. Her philosophy for business growth is to lead with value and stand out from the crowd. Her simple strategy makes it easy for nurse entrepreneurs and hospices to set themselves up as "the only logical choice."

She resides in rural Northeast Kansas on a small homestead with her husband, Greg, their livestock and honey bees. To learn more about her course, "How To Get Doctor's Offices Begging You To Learn More About Your Business," visit her website at https://hospicemarketingmaven.com/page/teresa-sanderson

8

DANELLE'S STORY

If you could have seen my face when I was asked if I was going to be a part of this book…

I was like a deer in headlights. The thought running through my head was, "I am not a writer; what business do I have being a part of this book?" I took some time to look at what the meaning of this book was and what part I'd played in all the things … Then I took a hot minute and thought, "Yeah, why wouldn't I be a part of this book?"

I heard about Martha from my therapist (we'll get to that in a bit). She knew from working with me that I was embarking on a journey to start my own business. She let me know that Martha had just started a group to help entrepreneurs. I don't know about you, but when I have someone that I trust drop a name like that, I check it out. Little did I know that Martha would end up being not only my mentor, but also one of my dearest friends.

I went on a mission, and I found all the things Martha is about, strategies on how to work from home successfully, how to do everything from a heart-centered space, creating a seven-figure business from home, as well as her brilliance and, best of all, her transparency. Yeah, well, I'll just say that I turned a little stalker-like and binged on all things Martha. *wink* I know that if you are reading this book, you've done it too!

Not long after discovering her, I went all in on a business event that Martha was putting on for people in my area. I even pulled the trigger on the VIP ticket – front row, baby! It even came with a 1:1 session with her! I was stoked. I soaked up every single little detail during that event. I left there confident that I was going to make this happen, and she was the person that was going to teach me how. I wasn't wrong.

At the time of embarking on this journey, my kids were almost raised. I'd been in a job that I wasn't in alignment with for sixteen very long years. To be totally honest with you, I was a miserable soul. The job was sucking the life out of me. I went into therapy to fix my test anxiety, you know, hazards of the job, and I discovered I was a hot mess.

This therapy was hard core, all in, get my sh*t figured out therapy. I discovered that guilt was driving me—I was in the muck of existence that people can fall into when they just accept what life offers through your typical nine to five job. I mean, my home life was great. I had a wonderful husband, and my kids were growing up to be successful people, but the anxiety and stress from this job was tearing me all the way down.

The guilt kept talking and talking loudly. I was hearing myself say things like, "But you have a good job, you've got sixteen years in, you are almost up to four weeks paid vacation, the benefits are great, you can't get good medical insurance if you leave here; just stop it, you are blessed." But I just wasn't in alignment with my purpose.

My anxiety level that was off … the … charts. It took everything I had to hold myself together during my workday. I would find myself in the bathroom just to escape the misery I was in. It was my break away from it all, the one place I found that I could breathe air fully into my lungs. My health was taking a toll, and I was soon faced with having to decide between a good job or my physical and mental health. This was affecting every aspect of my life by now. Even the good parts.

Through therapy and hard work, I began to gain more confidence. I was even starting to believe in my dreams. I was feeling like I could maybe even take a chance on myself. It was during this time that Martha and I were getting to know each other more. I'm telling you; this relationship was God's nudge.

I scheduled my 1:1 time with Martha, and it was there that I was able to share with her all my dreams about my business and my family. I shared my vision and my plans to make it happen, and we created a plan to work on that together.

Soon after this, she came to me with a business opportunity. I was so scared. What she offered me was so far out of my element that my brain was all over the place; I'd be lying if I didn't say there was some anxiety there too. My heart told me to trust her, even if I had to do it scared. I jumped into that opportunity with her, right then and there.

All of this brought something for me to look forward to. I was defining my new direction and learning so much about myself. My natural skills began to shine through even when I may have still been confused on my direction. I would express this to Martha, and her reply was always, "I've got you."

I've got you. What does that even mean? I was leaning in, though; my heart knew I could trust her. See, it's the plan, the little nudges that I kept on following. I mean, come on, we all know how God uses Martha and her giving heart for the good of ALL people! I listened, and I followed.

I was really beginning to let go of the fear after seeing that I had people on my side that believed in me. After a lot of soul searching and prayer, I decided that it was time to walk away from my job. I did that scared, too.

I continued to work the plan of building my business. Things were going along so smoothly; I was finding my happy place, and my anxieties were easing. I was beginning to love life. Then, it happened. Another pivotal time in this part of my journey … COVID-19.

Most everyone was being sent home to work. My husband was no exception to that rule. We were thankful he was still able to continue to work. His income was carrying our household while I built my business. The plan was to take the next five years in the building phase, so I could support us, and my husband could then retire. Five years, that's all I needed.

You know about those best laid plans though, right? Our world came crashing down around us. That leap of faith that I'd taken in leaving my job for my health and giving up a great income to make it all happen crashed. My husband was forced to retire due to cutbacks in his company. Devastation hit us hard. The income that was carrying us would soon be gone!

I had put my trust in feeling like I could step away from the security of a job to serve through my heart, and now, my hopes of traveling the world while we were still young enough to travel vanished also. Just like that … gone. The questions all led to "What are we going to do now?"

God knew. He was putting us in the exact position that he needed us in. The timing was perfect. By allowing myself to trust and let go of my own plan, he put my family in a place of service. Our world changed in ways we could have never dreamed of. Not only was he showing me how I could shift a career path, but there was a place that I was needed.

It was in this time that Martha reached out and asked me to be a part of her business team. Not just her MLM team, but her business! What? You want *me*? That "I've got you" that she kept mentioning was happening in the moment. The abundance of what God can deliver was being realized in that instant. This woman has a heart of gold, y'all, and the realization that she wanted ME beside her on this journey ... you're dang straight I jumped for joy at this opportunity.

HBR is what happened next, and Martha was right ... this was BIG! It has delivered the life that I dreamed of— the empowerment of bringing our families back home by choice, to create a life on our terms, to provide well for our families and to give our family the gift of time. I, again, wake up every single day feeling blessed in this life; my heart is now aligned with my purpose.

Now it's your turn ... are you ready?

ABOUT DANELLE

Danelle Fowler is a Business Strategist, Mindset Coach, wife, mom, and proud grandma. She courageously left corporate America to protect her mental and physical health and now serves alongside Martha Krejci as COO of Martha Krejci Company to impact the lives of women entrepreneurs all over the planet.

Danelle has a heart to serve women who are highly sensitive in order to help them overcome their big emotions. She is passionate about seeing these women embrace their sensitivity and pursue thriving, harmonious, and passion driven lives. She excels in leadership and process management, and her organizational skills are unmatched. She is certified in Tapping and Content Creation, and is currently pursuing certification in Conscious Language, Sacred Body Language, and Neurolinguistic Programming.

Connect with her at http://danellefowler.com/quicklinks

9

AMY W'S STORY

I woke up and immediately knew something was wrong. Can your face "fall asleep" like an arm or a leg? One look in the mirror, and I knew my face wasn't asleep - I looked like I'd had had a massive stroke. That moment of shock in 2002 at thirty-six years old—the breath-taking concern for my two small children that washed over me in a sweaty instant—started a journey of healing and transformation that elevated my life and defined my resilience. We have all had moments that alter our world forever. Who knew I'd be grateful for that challenge—and the financial challenges that followed—because they showed me a road map that I can share with you?

You do not have to figure all this out by yourself. You are not alone. My path took years and led us to two six-figure incomes in one year! The road was paved with a lot of mistakes and false starts, and I learned by doing and failing. I'm here to share what I learned, so you can avoid those same mistakes and start to live your life in balance and in service.

What is Bell's Palsy anyway? Well, my friend, it is when one side of your face is paralyzed. Not asleep, paralyzed. Technically, it is weakness of the facial muscles as the result of inflammation of the seventh cranial nerve. It affects about 40,000 people in the United States every year. Many people fully recover.

What was it like? I could not smile. I could not eat easily. Drinking from a glass was a no-go for months. I sported a lovely eye patch for nine months because my eye was unable to close. That meant adding ointment directly to my eye (can you say yuck? I did!), taping it closed, and wearing an eye patch 24/7 because sleep with one eye open is just an expression. I missed having depth perception and peripheral vision. Life went on. I was determined not to let this slow me down or stop me. I used humor and sheer guts to push through and focus on what was truly important—my family. As you can imagine, there is so much more to that part of my story, but what I want to focus on today is how it seared into my heart the importance of faith, health, and resilience.

One of the best pieces of advice I ever received was to not wait for that emergency, that heartbreak, or that accident to happen. Get prepared NOW! Sounds great, right? But what does it mean to be prepared? For me, that meant having the means to manage whatever life might have lined up for my family and me. Means aren't always financial. We all need mental strength, spiritual fortitude, and physical health. These are the foundation of all our other efforts. I felt I had those well in hand despite Bell's palsy—I just needed to figure out that pesky financial piece. Now, let me be clear. I am grateful for all the incredible blessings I have received throughout my life. I have always had my basic needs met. I do not take that for granted. We can be grateful for our blessings and still struggle.

I remember walking into Ikea to shop for college furniture,

praying that the three hundred dollars I had to spend would cover what was needed. I have opened credit cards to help with bills. I have failed financially. Call it optimism that I just always believed that if we weren't extravagant, if we did the right things, it would always work out. Well, folks, hope is not a strategy! College degrees, work in the non-profit world at the COO and executive director level, and all the service in the world did not add up to work that paid well enough for my family to live free of financial worry. What to do?

I figured I would start a business, a side hustle. I mean, look at how successful people can be with their in-home businesses. There are so many great companies with so many great products, so I tried it. The first business I tried never took off financially, and I learned so much from generous mentors and met incredible people who enriched my life and still hold places in my heart. My second attempt helped transform my health because, believe it or not, I got Bell's Palsy a SECOND time in 2017. I'm still loving that business, and it is WHY I am healthier today than I have ever been. I made the choice to go all in and was growing that in-home business when my husband was laid off from his job in April of 2020.

Talk about a moment in time that makes your heart race and your hands sweat. The world was shut down, literally. Our income and health insurance were gone after years of building a business we expected to retire from way down the road. We leaned on our mental strength our spiritual fortitude and looked at our options. My business didn't cover the bills. My business did, however, lead me to someone who completely transformed our lives.

You know those trainings we come across? I would typically think that maybe this one will help me elevate my business to where it can support our family! Well, Home-Based Revolution isn't about that. It is about creating multiple streams of business, sharing resources, and leading not only your family, but all families, out of the financial darkness into a different kind of way to live. Stay with me—I totally get the "huh" feeling you are having right now because I had it too. I just knew this had worked for my mentor, Martha Krejci, and it was working for members of her community. So we took a deep breath, we got help from our family, and we pivoted. Two new businesses were born that week, and in less than a year, they were both making six figures. It took an incredible amount of personal work, extraordinary deep digging, and more than one come-to-Jesus moment to realize I wasn't thinking big enough. You see, Martha has an ironclad determination to free families from financial woes by sharing her skillset, and she is on a mission to make families invincible. How could we just think about our family? What could we do? What could we share that would help lead other families to freedom?

Surely this answer involved years of research, planning, education, and hard work? Surprise! Our biggest blessing, which is the easiest to share with others, came from a random conversation and a follow-up phone call. Can you believe it? It all started with notarizing real estate documents. My husband would help get documents signed a few times a month starting in 2010. When he needed help, I jumped in and learned the ropes. Over the years, we developed a system that we use for every single closing. Sharing that journey and system so others can do the same thing is our mission. That was the beginning of one of the most enjoyable, simple, inspiring ways to help others while earning enough to truly support our family.

What about the second business? My husband opened his own firm in the same line of work, but he based his in service and connection. He can offer burned out, tired, overworked people in his field a completely different way to do things. I always believed success would be found in the grind. Hard work leads to rewards. Home-Based Revolution turned that concept on its head! Life is short. You might wake up tomorrow and not be able to smile. When we left behind the grind and focused on service, everything changed. You can do the same thing.

My story didn't go according to plan – sound familiar? I worked with no balance and less income than my family needed for years. I struggled to protect my health and heal. I needed someone to show me a better way. I found a mentor with a heart for service who shared her path in order to illuminate possibilities for others. YOU don't need a college degree. You don't need years to build. You are where you are with what you need at this moment. I'll forever be grateful that Martha shared her experience and knowledge with me – so you better believe I'm going to pay it forward and share with you! Are you ready? Let's go!

ABOUT AMY W.

Amy Wicks-Horn is a recovering non-profit executive whose journey to resilience began in 2002 when she woke up one morning with the right side of her face completely paralyzed! She had Bell's Palsy.

Who knew she would be grateful for that challenge – and the financial challenges that followed - because they showed her a road map to resilience and success that she now shares with others in her mission to help people take control of their finances and their health.

As a mother, wife and community volunteer Amy simply shares what worked for her in the hopes that it can help others. If you are ready to leave the grind behind to find balance while earning the income your family needs check out Amy's free resources at amywickshorn.com

10

MEGAN'S STORY

Do you ever feel like you are stuck in a box with the lid on? You can't even see your way out. You hear other people on the outside of the box, and they seem like they are having the time of their life, but how on earth are you going to get out of this box? For me, the box I was in was financial burden. The walls of the box were built by following all the rules of what society said to do to be successful and live financially free. The more I implemented their strategy – go to college, get a fancy degree, have a nine to five career – the more the walls of the box caved in on me.

Staring at the lid that was out of reach had me questioning my personal belief if I could ever get out of the box. What is your box? Financial burden? Working a stressful job? Wanting to serve others in a heart-centered way? Deeply longing to be at home with your children homeschooling them, but you have to show up to a nine to five to support them? Or maybe your box is knowing that others have had success working from home, and how can you believe it's for you when the walls keep caving in?

I found myself in a career I loved, but the income potential was directly tied to hours worked. You show up to work, you get paid. There was no possibility of increasing the income unless more hours were worked. You work these hours, and you get paid this amount of money. There was a lid on my capacity to earn money. That right there was suffocating. I refused to spend my moments making impact with my career at the expense of my family. It was gut wrenching knowing someone was in need and I was unable to give generously.

Network marketing was the big craze. It was a way out of trading hours for dollars. I had been stepping into the ring of social selling for several years. It was fun, getting to know people, seeing people walk in freedom with products that serve them, and watching the work dig our family out of the student loan debt. There was slow progress, but it was moving until the world came to a halt in 2020.

The system that I had been using and was being taught was limited to face-to-face interaction. I was done. Done hustling, done striving, done pushing the walls of the box. Ready to throw in the towel. Have you ever been ready to give up in what seems like the final round of the fight only to have someone come in the rink with you, give you a drink, and say, "Come on, girl; I know you can do it! I'm here to fight with you! Let me show you the way!" The woman who stepped into the ring was Martha Krejci. She was lifting the lid and shoving the walls down on my box.

Martha was teaching a system on how to have multiple income streams from home. It was like she attached a string to the top of the box from the outside and pulled the thing open with her programs and coaching and step by step instructions on how to craft a heart-centered business from home while showing up in service to others. It was no longer limited to only certain people achieving success working from home, but instead, it was a "let me show you step by step how to actually do the thing." I began to have hope again that it was possible to show up in service to others in a way that was unique to my personal giftings.

Something marvelous happens when Martha steps into the ring. The game changes! Suddenly, you have someone saying, "Punch here, now duck, step right, lift your chin." There is strategy to the entire thing. What once seemed like walls caving in was now endless potential. There was a moment when working with Martha in a group coaching setting that asking a question revealed a limiting belief I was holding onto. There was no shame, no pressure, just open spaces to process what was going on and a take-my-hand approach at walking forward out of the lies.

No one had ever held space for me like she did in a business setting before. There was no shaming. No "You just need to get over it; no, we don't have time for that here." It was a gentle nudge out of that space and bringing the dark into light. She removed the walls by holding space for all of life circumstances I had faced that brought me to that moment in time, hungry to learn and chained back by lies that were once said. Martha was showing me something so impactful. When we hold space for others, we are actually reaching our hand back into the fire from the place we once had been and saying, "Come on, girl; this is the way."

In Home-Based Revolution, we learn that the very thing that was trying to take us out is the same thing that we are called to help others overcome. As a young girl, I can remember saying I wanted to wear a bikini. The words spoken back to me in that moment left an imprint on my heart forever. "Little girls your size shouldn't wear a bikini. Nobody wants to see your belly. We need to cover it up." Those were lies that were spoken over me at only five years old. I didn't know the difference between the truth and a lie. Shame came over me like a wet heavy blanket weighing me down.

The pressure of the world that says "achievements equal worthiness" had me raising my hand to far too many things, trying to earn love without rejection. I can control the rejection based on being the best. Hustling for all the worthiness had me needing comfort, and food was always an open cabinet away. Have you ever done that? Said yes to far too many things and used food to comfort what was going on in your heart from the pressure of it all?

As Martha was in the ring, teaching me how to create multiple streams of income from home, I stepped into the ring of helping women strip away the lies they have been believing about themselves that were using food as a counterfeit comfort. Their identity as a child of God is restored, and they walk in freedom from the bondage of using food as a counterfeit comfort. It's time women stop hiding in shame from what God called "very good." No longer are we trying to become something by checking off all the boxes. We are fully seen and deeply loved, and from that place, we go do the work of the Lord.

ABOUT MEGAN

Megan Dale is a Pediatric Physical Therapist, a Revelation Wellness Fitness Instructor, and a Trim Healthy Mama Coach.

She teaches women how to transform their life from the bondage of striving and slimming their bodies to be worthy of love. She helps women that struggle with poor body image and break the chains of an unhealthy relationship with food from the pressure of life that has been put on them or that they have put on themselves. She simplifies the process into easy does it, actionable steps because trying harder only has you trying again and again. It all starts by learning how to have slimming desserts for breakfast.

She helps moms with daughters be able to get out of the body shaming cycle and into freedom. While they are getting free, she teaches them the tools so their daughters can stay free. Imagine what it would have been like having someone show you the pathway to freedom.

Connect with her at https://withmegandale.com/links

11

CAROLYNN'S STORY

I was made to be a mom. I'm one of those weird people who knew from a very young age that I wanted to be a mom. I loved playing "house" as a young child. My mom did home daycare for thirteen years of my life, so I grew up around a lot of kids. I've always been drawn to children, and I had my first "paid" babysitting job when I was eight. Don't be scared; I'm pretty sure I wouldn't let my kids babysit that young. The grandma of the baby I watched was home, but she was busy getting ready for work. I lived in the townhouse right next door, and my mom was always home during that time, too. I literally just held the baby while watching the TV show *Funhouse*, and I got paid for it! Man, did I think I was hot stuff, but it instilled a confidence in me from a very early age that I was good with kids. Because of my mom's job, I had an abundance of babysitting opportunities. I was always babysitting and was even a nanny for a couple of families over the summers. I also worked at an athletic club, and I taught swimming lessons, worked in the childcare center, and was a birthday party facilitator during high school. My considerations of careers all centered on how easy they would be to fit around family life and having children. I thought about physical and occupational therapy and teaching. I struggled in physics and chemistry, so I set my sights on teaching. In college, I worked at a daycare center and majored in elementary education and minored in early childhood.

Two weeks after my college graduation, I got married (I had a plan for my life, and I was in a hurry to bring it to fruition). Three months after getting married, we got pregnant with our first. Even though I had more experience than most, I was shocked at how terrified I was to bring him home. Six months after he was born, we were pregnant again. When we had our third child, our oldest wasn't three yet. Our fourth came twenty-one months after our third. I remember coming up on my thirtieth birthday and being sad that it was going to be so long until I held another baby (thinking about grandkids). I had always wanted four kids (seriously had names picked out before I even met my husband), but I had never fathomed that I'd be done having children by the time I was thirty. Luckily, God had other plans and blessed us with two more children over the next seven and a half years. So there I was, living my dream. I was a mom, everything I had ever dreamed of. I had made children my identity. They were my purpose for being on this Earth.

My dreams had come true! But it wasn't what I'd expected. I didn't feel fulfilled like I had imagined, and I certainly wasn't as good of a mother as I had anticipated either. This wasn't how it was supposed to be. Now, I'm not saying I don't love my children, because I do. I love them fiercely. I believe almost every parent loves their child(ren) unconditionally. I love my kids, I'm so grateful for my kids, we are truly blessed. But why did I feel deflated, unfulfilled, and dissatisfied in motherhood? Why was motherhood so hard? I mean, I was prepared; I knew what I was getting into. I had a lot of practice and experience. But I was tired. I wasn't taking good care of myself, so losing my patience became a habit. I started seeing my kids react and treat each other the same way. It's amazing how children are incredible imitators; they are like mirrors, and I was always taken aback when they would reflect my ugliness back at me and to their siblings.

Realizing that motherhood wasn't all fulfilling and not my sole purpose made me feel like a failure. How could I be so bad at the thing I know God had created me for? Through some wise counsel, I came to realize that I was actually being very unfair to my children. It was completely unrealistic of me to think that humans could fulfill me. That's not my children's job. Coming to terms with this fact made me start to search and open my eyes. I don't want to be debilitated by an empty nest like my mother was. I needed to find another purpose outside of my children. I needed to find some way I could still serve and have positive impact, now and after my children leave the nest. I know in my head that motherhood is the most important work I will ever do; however, it's hard for my heart to feel it, especially on the hard days.

I started looking for things I could do. I tried paper crafting and joined an MLM (multi-level marketing) company associated with such products. I liked it, but I wanted something where I could have more impact. I wanted to be able to serve and really impact lives. I tried a more health-associated MLM and loved it at first, but it's kind of fizzled out. I don't put in the time and make it a big enough priority to be successful at it. There are many times I've felt like a failure, and I really just don't like the "ickiness" that seems to be synonymous with people's mindsets when it comes to MLMs. The community of the MLM is fantastic, and I also joined a Mom's Day Out program with some amazing ladies. This moms community has become my community. My last two children's godparents have come from the group. They are my "in real life" lifeline.

Then, COVID. Mom's Day Out could no longer meet, Bible studies could no longer be held. Community was so hard to come by. I started looking online for a heart-centered group. One of my MLM friends recommended Martha Krejci's group; at the time, it was called "Heart-Centered and Successful Moms." This is what I was looking for! Hopeful, I jumped in with two feet. The community was so great, I ended up joining Martha's program and eventually joined Change Makers. Change Makers is my "business" community. They are there to cheer me on and remind me to grant myself grace when things take longer than I want them to. This group understands my desire to be more than "just a mom" and to serve in other ways than motherhood. I have rediscovered that my purpose can be motherhood, but it can also be in serving other parents. Serving parents is something I'll be able to continue to do, even after my kids have left.

Martha has taught me how to serve without sacrificing my family priorities while still fulfilling my purpose outside of motherhood. I get to build a business around my family commitments. I took the leap of faith and became certified to teach barre classes and as a life coach; these are two things that I thought I'd pursue after the kids were gone. Martha has given me so much hope that my purpose can be found and served through in different avenues. I had lost hope and felt like a failure because what I thought my purpose would look like had become completely different than I imagined. Martha opened my eyes to the many opportunities I was overlooking and even those that I did not know existed.

ABOUT CAROLYNN

Carolynn is first and foremost a child of God, a wife of seventeen years and mother of six. She has four boys and two girls ranging in ages from sixteen to four. She has a degree in Elementary Education and Early Childhood and taught preschool for five years before becoming a stay at home mom. Besides being a personal chauffeur to her children, she is also a Barre instructor, life coach, parent coach, author and course creator. Carolynn loves to help guide mothers to be the best mothers they can be and is passionate about helping moms go from feeling overly busy and stressed to balanced and blessed.

Connect with her at https://mylittlebitoflife.com/findcarolynn

1 2

CARRIE'S STORY

I think there comes a time in every person's life when they stop and wonder, is this it? Is this as good as it's ever going to get? There must be more to life than this hamster wheel I'm on, right? I asked myself that question time and again. As a midlife mom, I know I'm not alone. In fact, many have asked me that very same question.

I have a great husband and two pretty terrific kids, and yet, I am often restless, searching for "what's next" or a new adventure. I've been a missionary for over thirty years. In that time, I traveled to more than twenty-five countries and met people of all creeds, colors, and religions. No matter what continent or what language, one thing was consistent -- people underestimated their true value. Women in every country I worked in struggled with their self-worth and the ability to make themselves a priority. Over the years, I've had a lot of different jobs as well, yet I never really felt like I had found my thing. I was like so many of those women I met, and I realized the grass wasn't greener on someone else's continent or in someone else's culture. We all struggle ... I struggled.

I was unhappy. "Unhappy" sums it up but doesn't necessarily do it justice. I was living with chronic back pain, unable to put my own socks and shoes on. I had gained fifty pounds in what seemed like a short amount of time. At one point, I was sure I was going crazy. I couldn't remember anything. Common everyday words escaped me. It became a joke in my family. I'd refer to a restaurant as "the eat place" because the word "restaurant" just wouldn't come to me. I laughed with them on the outside, but inside, I was cementing the ugly things I seemed to tell myself every day. "There's something wrong with you, Carrie. You'll never be healthy, Carrie. You'll never be your ideal weight because you can't even put your shoes on yourself! You're a train wreck, and you'll never get anywhere. You have nothing of value to offer anyone." I hid it all behind a bright smile and enough talent for others to think I had it all together. Sound familiar?

What nobody saw, including my own family, was that I could barely get up in the morning. I didn't really see the point. I even sought out specialists to tell me what was wrong with me. Surely, there was a chemical imbalance in my brain, or I had a tumor or something, right? If there wasn't a medical reason, the alternative was something I didn't know how to face.

Before long, I knew I had slipped into a dark depression. I knew I had reached burnout at a job I had loved but had no support in and was treated terribly at. I did eventually quit that job, but even that was long overdue. I'm not a quitter, so it was very hard to walk away, and so much damage had already been done. What was I going to do now? I tried to talk to my husband about it, but unbeknownst to him, his reply shattered me. He said, "I don't know what you're gonna do now, but whatever it is, make more money than you we're making at the last jobs." Basically, what I heard him say and what settled in my heart in that moment was, "That job you almost killed yourself doing and were treated so badly at was a waste of time, and now I need you to step up."

I was at a total loss, but I knew I had some talent, so I decided to start my own business around my music and ministry. At times, my mission field was East Africa and Europe, and at other times, it was my kitchen and laundry room. Maybe I could build a business around the things and events that I loved doing. After working in over twenty different countries and then offering retreats and keynote speaking across the U.S., I knew I had potential. However, have you ever tried starting a business from a place of total loss? Total loss equaled no idea what I was doing. I tried a few things and saw some level of success but certainly nothing like I believe my husband was expecting. I was back to living in a state of "there's got to be something more," which had me, once again, on a hamster wheel, and the cycle continued.

I believe that many people, like me, know deep down inside that they were created for something greater. I knew it was possible to be successful. After all, other people had done it. So what was wrong with me? Why couldn't I crack the code? Maybe I just wasn't good enough or smart enough or savvy enough or talented enough ... maybe I just wasn't enough.

One thing I was, though, is persistent. I wasn't ready to give up on me yet. I knew I just needed help. I know it was divine intervention that I was introduced to the Home-Based Revolution, or HBR as we lovingly call this program. It started me on a journey that changed everything. Suddenly, the impossible seemed possible, the steps were simpler, the road map was legible, and my little spark of hope was ignited into a flame!

Martha Krejci knew what she was doing. When she began HBR, she required each of us to work on our mindset first and foremost. Some people complained about this step because they wanted to dive right into all the things, and let me tell you, there were a lot of things to dive into. However, mindset was where we all had to start, and I know beyond a shadow of a doubt that without it, I would not be where I am today. I know that I would still be sitting on the sidelines, believing the lie that I am not enough. Nothing that has the potential to change hundreds and thousands of lives ever starts with the phrase "I am not enough."

I'm a Christian, and for me, the story of the young boy with five loaves and two fish that fed the multitude is a perfect summary of HBR. I'm not saying Martha is Jesus, of course. However, just like Jesus was able to take the little bit that one person had and have it impact thousands and thousands of lives, God has given Martha the ability to teach us how to take our ideas, however small they might be, and turn them into a way for us to love and serve others while, at the same time, changing the trajectory of our futures forever.

In those months, before I decided to invest in myself through HBR, I never imagined that just over a year later, I would be creating courses that help people find their balance again, live their purpose and resonate joy. I founded Beautiful Balanced Living as a resource for those who also believe that there has got to be more to life. I created two signature programs using the tools I learned in HBR and the powerful framework of Oola, where I am now a certified life coach.

The Life Balance Bootcamp for Women and the sister course, Life Balance Bootcamp for Teens, is helping women (no matter their age) take control of their fitness, finances, and futures --

sometimes for the very first time. It gives them permission to prioritize their time and talent.

My passion is to help women see their BEAUTIFUL. It's not my goal to help them see that they ARE beautiful; that part comes naturally as they put in the work and effort to find their beautiful. I am not talking about an outward appearance that the world would see, although more often than not, there is a physical transformation too. The beautiful that I am referring to is found in the balanced life, the one that takes back control of finances and fitness, two areas where my clients often struggle the most. That builds up their confidence and faith again. The beautiful that describes their marriage and their relationship with their children. Please note, I said beautiful, not perfect. In fact, "perfect" has no place in my beautiful balance. There is only one perfect, and that is God.

Beautiful describes what is possible; it defines a life in balance. It's a feeling in your bones that only comes when you are walking in purpose, free from perfection and filled with your worth. You can build a beautiful life on purpose, with purpose, and for a purpose. HBR gave me tools to do just that. For that, I am forever grateful.

ABOUT CARRIE

Carrie is a builder of beautiful. Her passion is inspiring women of all ages to reconnect to their true beauty and divine purpose.

She is a keynote speaker, retreat leader and a missionary of 31 years. Carrie has shared her music, message and mentoring with audiences in over 20 countries across the global.

This singer/songwriter, wife, military momma and life coach from the Buffalo, NY area is is the founder of Beautiful Balanced Living and creator of the Life Balance Bootcamp for Women and Teens. Her mission is to eradicate hopelessness by providing a simple blueprint to beautiful.

Connect with Carrie https://bit.ly/CarrieConnect

LINDA'S STORY

I remember sitting at my grandmother's desk "playing business" with old ledgers and bank slips. As a young child, I always had an interest in money and business. I was the kid selling lemonade, running a yard sale, or coming up with fundraising ideas. Some might say it was in my blood.

But somewhere along the line, I got fed the lie that pursuing money wasn't "good." I began feeling ashamed to share my thoughts and plans in fear that someone might think I was "greedy" or "loved money." It didn't matter my reason or what I wanted to do with the money, I couldn't take the risk. You see, I have always been the good one, the one who followed the rules, made the right choice, played it safe ... you get the picture. I strived to make everyone else happy, even at the sacrifice of my own wishes. Yes, indeed, I was a people pleaser, although I would never admit it. Even now, as I type, I want to press delete.

Growing up, I wasn't a spender; I was a natural saver. I remember going on vacation, and everyone else came back with lots of stuff, but me? Just a calendar. My knowledge of money at a young age was limited, but I knew the value of money and, more importantly, the value of having it for a rainy day. My mom was a single mother until I was eight, and even after she remarried, they had their own money ups and downs. I observed as they worked hard and maneuvered those changes. I witnessed all the emotions from joy and excitement to stress and frustration. I am thankful for this and the perspective it provided me.

When I got married, we both had student loans, so we implemented a plan to get them paid off and become debt free. Then came a mortgage, car payment, two children, and well, life happens. We made some smart choices and some mistakes along the way. It many ways, we had dreams bigger than our income.

There was so much we desired to do with and for our family, so many we wanted to help and serve. You know that moment sitting in church or talking to a friend, and you hear of a family that has been through a tragedy or a cause hits your heart so close to home, and you want so badly to do more to help. You give what you can and say someday … someday, I'll be able to do more. There it is again. The desire to have more money. not for the sake of having money but to help others and create a better life for your family.

When my children were toddlers, we facilitated a financial program in our home and at church. I fell in love with the process of helping people evaluate and get control of their finances. I totally geeked out when chatting about budgets, money, goals, dreams, and how to get there. I found my happy place, where it wasn't taboo to talk about money. But you can't earn money doing that, or so I thought.

Over the next twelve years, I attempted a few business ideas. I would dive in, but soon, the doubts and that old feeling of shame would creep back in, pushing out the excitement and motivation. My husband and children would support and encourage me, but the turmoil came from within.

Looking back, I can see all the signs of self-sabotage. I was getting in my own way; old beliefs and fears would mess with my head. I struggled with doubt, limiting beliefs, fear of failure, probably fear of success, too. I unknowingly allowed procrastination and lack of consistency to thwart any positive effort I tried to make because my mindset produced those negative behaviors.

Then, the excuses came.

That plan was impossible anyway, this goal was unrealistic, that business was too much of a risk, I should be focusing on my family, I need to learn to be content and stop these crazy endeavors. Now, don't get me wrong, I would see some monetary success, but nothing near what I was truly capable of until …

I joined a program that I thought would teach me how to better grow the business I currently was building, which I did in a way I never dreamed of, but it was so much more.

Having Martha Krejci as a coach and mentor affected not just my business, now businesses, but also the deep stuff, the stuff that really matters.

Breaking mental blocks that I did not even know existed, my mindset has been forever changed. The funny thing is I was the person that said I don't need the mindset stuff; I have goals, just show me the steps. I wanted to jump in, take action, and make it happen. But when what you are doing isn't working and you don't know why, you need someone to guide you and help you course correct. And now, I am teaching mindset to my financial coaching clients, so they can get out of their own way, too!

We can't change the past, but we can change the way we process it, allow it to affect us, and learn from it. We need to embrace our past experiences and choices, our choices and the choices made by others that affected us, if we are to change who we are today and where we want to go in the future. This and so much more I learned, thanks to Martha.

What a difference one year can make in mindset, goals, and finances. Building my business sustainably with balance and from a heart of serving others provides me the opportunity to grow on many levels -- mentally, emotionally, spiritually, and, of course, financially.

I can grow a business, homeschool my teenagers, focus on my relationship with my husband, and serve my community without falling prey to feelings of guilt, shame, and frustration because I have a mission and purpose, I know who I am, and, most importantly, WHO created me.

Possessing the support and knowledge that I need to make things happen has empowered me to step into a place that I can serve others with the gifts, talents, and vision that God has given me. I'm still a little scared and unsure at times, but I know I have the tools and support from my family, my mentor, and my community that I need to not let it paralyze me.

As a financial coach, I help families take back their lives, create a legacy. The fact is that money is not evil; it is an amplifier that allows good people to do more good. When people fear wealth, are drowning in debt, or just don't have a plan, what they can accomplish and contribute is severely limited. I am breaking down those walls around the topic of money to empower families to do more, give more, and serve more.

George S. Clawson wrote in his book *The Richest Man in Babylon*, "Our prosperity as a nation depends upon the personal financial prosperity of each of us as individuals." While I agree this is true, I would like to take it a step further and apply it to God's kingdom. The way I see it, there are many people who desperately want to do more, give more, and serve more but feel their hands are tied; they are strapped financially. My mission is to set the church free and empower believers who have given up their passions to pay the bills, believers who have dreams bigger than their paychecks, like I did.

After months of coaching families, I am launching my first course, Faith-Based Financial Freedom Revolution, allowing me to serve more families. It enables believers to follow their God-given passions to effect change in their family, their community, and their world. I meet families wherever they are at and walk with them the entire way.

My family is committed to this journey; we are planning our next steps of serving in ministry, traveling, and meeting needs that the Lord brings to us. We have begun the process of getting trained to work with a disaster relief ministry serving those whose lives have been turned upside down due to natural disasters. We will be in the position that we can give financially and physically go whenever the need arises. No longer will I have to sit there and wish I could give more, dream of the day I could go and help; we will be able to be there.

In addition to our current giving, we are building towards a monthly budget fund for random giving as the Lord leads us. Oh, the fun we will have blessing people!

What dreams has God placed in your heart?

ABOUT LINDA

Linda is LEO wife, homeschooling mama of two teens, entrepreneur, financial coach, speaker, and lover of natural things! As a self-proclaimed NERD (never ending reading diva) she believes that you should never stop learning, dreaming, and achieving.

With over 12 years' experience of helping people with their finances and her own family's journey, Linda is also the creator of the Faith-based Financial Freedom Revolution.

She is passionate about helping families achieve financial freedom so that they can do more, give more, and serve more enabling them to fulfill anything the Lord puts on our hearts. Her mission is to set the church free by empowering believers to honor God with their finances, take back their purpose, and serve like no other.

If you are ready to launch your faith-based financial freedom and create a legacy visit https://lindamaymyers.com/hello

1 4

DEE'S STORY

"You're too sensitive." Those words of judgement pierced my soul over and over. My gentle nature and huge open heart, combined with being very much in tune to the energies and emotions of those around me, was not viewed with appreciation as a gift. Rather, it was viewed as a flaw, a deficiency, something to fix.

So I did my best to swallow all emotions except for happy. I stuffed it all down and plowed through life. My job was to make sure others were happy at all costs. Because I was so in tune to other's energy and emotions, I became the ultimate fixer.

This became my greatest asset. I was a corporate professional and knew my stuff. They called me "the diplomat" for how I handled and navigated the stickiest situations and issues. I brought teams together, smoothed over conflict, and won over the most difficult customers. They gave me the riskiest projects with multiple projects running at the same time, each with huge budgets and diverse teams. Yet with all that, when it came to certain relationships, I crumbled. I stood face to face with corporate giants and held my own at work, but in other relationships, I was locked in fear.

I felt lost, frustrated, tired, and terribly sad.

Allowing others' unhealthy behaviors while stuffing my emotions down with a smile on my face showed up as lifelong guts issues, severe joint and muscle pain, nightmares, insomnia, and a host of other issues as my body screamed to get me to pay attention. More than one medical professional told me if I didn't figure out how to express my emotions, it would take its toll. Eventually, that's exactly what happened. I hit a wall so hard I landed in ICU, fighting for my life. It was a turning point, one pivotal moment in my journey. Something had to change.

I learned about boundaries but couldn't actually do them. I was locked in fear; words got stuck in my throat. I didn't want to continue to stuff my emotions down, but I didn't know how to express them either. I had no tools, I had never learned how to express them, it didn't come naturally. I didn't even know how to feel them or what to do with them if I did notice them.

I read, no, I consumed, information -- books I'd read nearly thirty years prior, courses, more books, counselors, doctors. I learned to use my sense of smell as my superpower because of its unfiltered interaction with the emotion center of the human brain. This helped me stay grounded, present, find my voice and courage to speak up, face my fear, stand in my power.

I was finally able to get in touch with my emotions and speak my gentle voice true to my core values and gentle nature. I discovered myself as a person, as a human with real and authentic emotions. I learned how to feel the emotions and let them flow freely with gentle power.

Eventually, I was moved to get my aromatherapy certification and focused on building a practice focused on emotional healing. It brought me so much joy to empower others' emotional healing journey. My practice was slowly growing, very, very slowly.

I live in a tiny town in rural Pennsylvania. Rural life moves at a different pace than the places I'd known all my life. It was a bit of a culture shock with some major adjustments along the way. My practice was mostly one-on-one, meeting in coffee shops, local workshops at the library, and vendor events.

Then came a big challenge during 2020 when things around the world shifted. I mean, how can I possibly help empower others' emotional healing using our sense of smell if we're not face to face? I'd only ever known and been taught in-person workshops and 1:1 face-to-face consultation. The foundation of what I did involved human interaction and dialog as we worked to find the right combination and profile that would best suit their emotional healing needs. For months, I struggled, did my best to offer consultations online. My tiny aromatherapy practice was slowly grinding to a halt. I was frustrated and terribly sad.

How in the world does a virtual aromatherapy practice function without smellevision?

At a time when the entire world needed emotional support and healing, here I was with tools to help but no way to spread the message. One day, I saw a YouTube video, and the woman speaking was speaking to me. Straight to my heart. It was like she was in my head. I told my husband, Tony, "It's like she can read my mind." As I shared with him over the next few days my "interactions" with this person named Martha Krejci, Tony was under the impression that she was consulting with me live. That's how real she spoke to me. By then, he was used to me interacting with people via video conference. Except this Martha person wasn't live, I was watching her recorded videos on social media. She was that good. She knew me, even though we hadn't met, and what she said clicked. It made perfect sense. She was a business strategist who shared freely and spoke from her heart right to my heart.

Meanwhile, Tony was on hold with his blue-collar work and, quite frankly, had no desire to return to it anytime soon. It was grueling, in all sorts of weather, and it was taking its toll on his body physically. His business was growing, profitable, but was so not what he wanted to be doing with his life. He's a musician, an amazing musician at that. He sits at the piano and composes his music right then and there, straight from his heart into the strings of his baby grand. When he plays, we will never hear it again unless he chooses to develop the piece and record it.

"Do you think I can do something online with my music?" he asked me. "Ha, I don't see how," I chuckled. He had performed at retirement homes and restaurants in the past, but everything was closed at this time. Then, it all started to fall into place.

I joined forces with hundreds of others creating a Home-Based Revolution with Martha leading the way. Within the first few days, I returned to Tony and told him I knew what to do. We set him up to play live music and share his talent with the entire world. He's met people from around our precious planet and has even played internationally. People from around the world tune in to listen to his music. His heart is full, and for the first time, he knows, really knows, it's not just me who loves the music pouring out of his soul.

I developed online courses to help others with emotional healing, empowered growth, and gentle boundaries. I learned specific aromatherapy techniques based in neuroscience, and my practice is now entirely virtual. It's a gentle step-by-step process to clear negative thoughts, feelings or memories that interfere with our sense of identity, and our limiting beliefs. My clients are from all over our beautiful planet earth - from Hawaii to

Netherlands. It blows my mind the people who are empowered by my message to heal and grow.

This emotional healing journey has been a journey of over thirty years. Finally, I hit my emotional stride in my early fifties. Looking back, I wish I had someone in my thirties and forties to come alongside me and share emotional insight. I wish I knew how a gentle soul could have simple boundaries. Someone to show me how to be in touch with my emotions and heed their beautiful message. Someone to show me how our emotions are a precious gift from our creator and are full of power, gentle power. Now, I reach back into the fire with my hand extended to anyone like me who feels locked in fear and just desires peace from deep within their soul. I help others discover their gentle boundaries, emotionally heal, and empower their massive growth. I'm on a journey and invite you to come alongside and join me.

ABOUT DEE

Dee Castelli is a wife, artist, poet, blogger, course creator and entrepreneur. She is passionate about empowered growth, emotional healing and gentle boundaries. As a Personal Coach and Certified Aromatherapist she empowers others to choose peace, claim their full life and live to their fullest potential. She absolutely loves helping others clear away overwhelm, frustration, fear and emerge with clear direction. If you're ready to claim your full life, join her at https://deecastelli.com/familybook so you can feel emotionally equipped to do all the things.

15

LEAH'S STORY

When I was a teenager growing up, you could say I was not on track to be what you would consider, in today's terms, to be successful. In fact, the opposite was true. A "statistic" was probably a better word to describe where I was headed in life.

I grew up in a fatherless home, I was a victim of child sexual abuse, and my mother had struggles with addiction from her own past trauma. As a result, she was not very present in my upbringing. As far as success goes, the outlook was just not looking good.

When I was fourteen years old, I met my future husband, Tyrone. He had also grown up in a dysfunctional environment. He grew up in a fatherless home with a mother who had her own set of issues.

We were glued at the hip from the beginning. Two functionally dysfunctional kids is what I always called us because we always had good intentions as far as what we wanted to do in life. We knew we wanted to be successful, but we had no idea how to get there and made many mistakes along the way.

Our definition of success changed over the years. In the beginning, we thought success meant having a good job with steady income because neither of our mothers had that. So that was the goal initially—get a job good and become contributing citizens in society and not dependent on the government.

My husband, who was my boyfriend at the time, was able to secure what we considered a good job at a fairly young age, and that job even included benefits. He got a job through the state and made over ten dollars an hour. He did that and school for the first several years of our relationship, and we thought we were very secure with that.

Because of that perceived security and our dysfunction, I felt very comfortable starting our own family. When I was eighteen years old, I became pregnant with our first daughter, Azaria.

Unfortunately, five months into that pregnancy, we found out the devastating news that she had a congenital heart defect that was incompatible with life. I made a very difficult decision to continue that pregnancy, knowing her life would be short but precious, and she lived with us here on earth until she was two months old. Her life, however, set the course for my own destiny as I chose to go to university and study the field of nursing.

While in school, we became pregnant with our rainbow baby, Niara. Our joy soon turned to sorrow as my mother lost her battle with addiction. Despite that joy and pain, I was able to still finish my degree in nursing.

We still didn't know much about success, but we thought we were on the right track by having a job and obtaining a degree. Our main goal, at the time, was to not be like our mothers. And I must specify, we loved our mothers. We understood they had incredible struggles beyond belief, and their lives were quite difficult. But our goal was to give our children more. We knew, even at a young age, that we wanted more, not only for our own children, but for our children's children.

Despite the odds against me, despite being that teenage mother and the daughter of an addict and poor and a nobody, I graduated from university with a degree in nursing. My boyfriend supported us while I did that.

When I earned my degree, it encouraged him to get his degree. He earned a degree in computer science, and we just really thought we had made it. We both had degrees and got jobs working in our respective fields and did well for many years. I even ended up going back for a master's degree and became a family nurse practitioner. We both became well respected in our fields, which is crazy to think about, considering where we came from.

But as the years went on and our now three children were growing up, we realized we were still paying off those student loans, and the credit card debt was not moving, despite the good income we were earning. We were just able to buy a house two years ago after working for several years. This was not the success we envisioned those many years ago. On paper, we looked very successful as we lived in a good neighborhood and had good jobs; yet, we had no savings and lived check-to-check for the most part. We did not have anything to leave for our children. In our minds, this was not the success we were we were dreaming of.

We knew there had to be more. We knew there had to be more purpose for our lives, but we just didn't know how to get there. I started researching other ways to build wealth and success outside of our fields, and that's when I came across a system that taught this exact thing -- how to think outside the box and look for other ways to build multiple streams of income.

Finding this system could not have come at a better time as I also deal with severe autoimmune issues. Dealing with these issues has reminded me why it is important to have a steady stream of passive income in the event I cannot work one day or just simply want to give my body the rest it needs.

It is a beautiful thing when you can find a community of women who all have this same goal as well, women who all want to leave legacies for their families. And to find a mentor who is willing to teach what they know is pure gold and very rare.

I realized our dreams of success could become a reality; our dreams of leaving a legacy for our children could become a reality, not just some pipe dream we had, and we're making it happen one step at a time.

Because I am a nurse practitioner and a patient, success, to me, means combining both of those into whatever income stream I am considering. My heart is serving people, especially those sick like me or those caring for those sick. I love encouraging fellow nurses to use their passions now in innovative ways. I also love to encourage patients to use their voice when talking to their providers. These ways of coaching are areas I never would have had the confidence to even consider if it wasn't for the cohort of women who have inspired me throughout the year. I have watched and learned from them.

The best part of this process is when my children ask what I am up to. They have literally said, "Hey, Mama, what business opportunity are you working on today?" or "Mom, how is the business going today?" Instilling these values into them at a young age is fulfilling a goal their father and I made so, so long ago. We are just beginning this journey really, and I cannot wait to see how it all ends.

ABOUT LEAH

Leah Parker is a true example of how God's grace can help one overcome even the most difficult situations.

She is married to her middle school sweetheart and is a mother to 3 living children and 1 angel in heaven.

She is also a Family Nurse Practitioner and currently travels throughout rural SC providing care for underserved patients.

She prides herself in providing a voice for the voiceless - encouraging and empowering patients to advocate for themselves. She is an autoimmune warrior and understands how frustrating the medical world can be.

In addition she gets great joy in helping other nurses and nurse practitioners who may be burned out rediscover and reinvigorate their passion for nursing and to use this passion for nursing innovation for better patient outcomes.

You can connect with her at https://withleahparker.com/page/learn-more

16

KORI'S STORY

It wasn't so long ago that life looked a lot different. It is hard to even think back to when the drinking was heavy and the dysfunction that goes right along with it was catastrophic. Everyday seemed like chaos. It was walking on eggshells in my own home, pretending things were okay in public, and numbing my pain through alcohol. I felt like a total failure, not knowing how I was going to change things.

Being in that head space just got me through the day and week, living for the weekend when I could get together with friends and blow off some steam, all while telling myself that I had solid relationships and the best friends a girl could ever ask for. What came with that life for me was fighting, hurt, and tons of hangovers. Still, I would wake up the next morning and start all over again.

I was lying to myself every step of the way. In reality, things were painful in every area of life. My relationships, my finances, my marriage, and my career. There was no balance, and my health suffered because of the amount of stress and pressure I put on myself by choosing to live that lifestyle. When you're in the middle of it, all you can see is that you're trying, trying so hard to get others to see where you are, who you are, and what you're made of, all the while feeling like a huge failure inside because you can't move past your limitations and self-loathing.

So the pattern continued to go round and round. And the inner chaos continued as well. I could never understand how everyone around me was succeeding. Or so it seemed. The view from the outside looks amazing because we tend to look at other people's lives through rose-colored glasses. All I could see was everyone else looking, healthy, happy, and financially secure. They were having fun on vacations, driving big boats and fancy cars. Pictures only showed the good times and laughter. I was in many of them myself. No one saw how the alcohol was running my life and ruining it at the same time.

I always had this little twinge, a nudge of sorts in the back of my mind, and it was consistent. Isn't there more to life than looking forward to Friday? Isn't there more than working in a dead-end job that doesn't even pay the bills, a place that will have my job reposted before my obituary is even written? What is my purpose? Was I just a number? This can't be all that I am meant for. There was always this pull inside me to be more, do more, and make more of an impact on the world. And no matter what seemed to be going on on the surface, this was the only feeling I couldn't shake. I was fighting an inner war with what I've been taught and what I felt like I was meant for. Society says have a good job, buy a house, get a boat, and learn to enjoy the limited time you have off. Be happy with what you are given, which was small bursts of time with family, and the rest of your life is spent trying to climb the corporate ladder just so you can afford to give your kids some kind of experience inside of those little time bursts.

I can remember sitting within the four walls of my cubicle at my desk, right after I was reprimanded by my boss for pushing back against the corporate policy, thinking to myself, "There has GOT to be more than this." I know I can do MORE than this. How can this be IT? I know there is a greater purpose to why I am here. But WHAT is it?

I always struggled working for "the man." I was labeled defiant, head strong, and rebellious. I was viewed as "the one that didn't follow the rules." And that, ultimately, cost me my steady employment, the best job I've ever had, according to society's standards. I was upset and relieved at the same time. The day I walked out of that job, I caught myself smiling in my review mirror. That memory has stuck with me. Why was that overwhelming feeling of freedom so potent? Instantly, the thought of, "Now I can do what I want," rushed over me. Now, I would make it BIG! This is my shot to make an impact and create the life I dreamed of. HA! HA! HA!

I failed. Not once but multiple times. And by multiple, I'm talking double digits! I spent the next seven years in and out of random jobs I hated, always let go for the same reasons. Defiant, doesn't follow rules, always questions authority, etc. Those were the terms used. Until finally, I knew that there was a reason I was coined rebellious by "the man." I was meant to cause waves and make a difference in the world. So that was just what I was going to do. But how? That was the question. I had made up my mind, and now, I needed to know how to do it. So I had one of my generalized conversations with God and said, "I surrender. Just show me the way. I am listening."

And then, it hit. That moment. The moment you knew that life would change forever. I had been watching this lady (aka Martha Krejci) on Facebook. She kept talking about making a sustainable living from home doing what you love. "Everything she says is gold," I kept thinking. I knew I had to find a way to get involved with this chick. I resonated with every word that came out of her mouth. It was like she was talking about me when she said, "I was born to disrupt."

MAN, me too, Martha, Me TOO! My next question to God was, "How can I afford this gold-filled opportunity?" I wasn't working, and obviously, I was still flailing around trying to figure it out, so to say that income was fruitful would be a laugh. I mean, I was nervous about where dinner was going to come from and how the mortgage was getting paid at that point. Then, one day, I was chit chatting with my mom on the phone, and she just randomly asked me, "Hey, have you heard of Martha Krejci?"

My mouth dropped open, and I squealed, "YES! I have been watching her for a while now. I just love her." We ended up having a long in-depth conversation about Martha's methods, and ultimately, we both wanted to take her course. My mom said to me, "I just don't have the time." And I replied with, "I have the time; I just don't have the money." This is the point where I am pretty sure God stepped in and gave her a nudge because she came back to me with, "How about I invest my money, and you invest your time?" I was FLOORED! It had barely been two days since I had asked God to pave the way. Of course, I instantly said yes and sent off that exciting first message to Martha, "Case Study."

When she came back to me and stated that she would honor the fifty percent off discount that had recently expired, I felt like I had won the lotto. And from that moment forward, I knew, life was never going to be the same. I knew, in my soul, that this was God's doing, and he had put her in my path for a reason. I was right! I immediately dove in with the eagerness of a five-year-old at a toy store. Everyone's pace is different. Some come in knowing who they want to serve and how they want to serve them. I went into HBR thinking I knew my purpose, and it wasn't until almost a year later I saw that I was way off base. Through this program, I learned so many things about myself, who I am and how I am called to serve others. I'm not going to sugar coat it. There were tears; I'm talking UGLY crying. There were fits of thinking I couldn't do it and almost throwing in the towel. But every time I thought of quitting, that little voice came back, "You were meant for more, Kori. You can do this. Keep going. You're almost there."

Then, one day, it hit me like a ton of bricks. My purpose was to change the world. I had to step into that space in order for God to work through me. And as soon as I did, "Grams Place" was born -- my way to give back to the community. I don't have it all figured out yet, but one day, you'll be driving down the street, and you'll see an amazing place in your community called Grams Place. Just know that was me. Be sure to stop in and experience the amazing atmosphere. Because everyone is home at Grams Place!

I've come to realize that without Martha, I would probably still be stuck in the same old rut. But since linking arms with her, my husband and I have both been sober for over a year, and in turn, everything in my life has changed. I've started multiple streams of income, found my purpose in life, and figured out how I am going to give back to the world and make massive impact.

My heart feels full. I will forever move forward in my growth because if I had given up all those years ago, I never would have found Martha. So, as you can see, before HBR, I was a wreck with no direction, no real purpose, just trying to get through life day by day, bottle by bottle, trying to numb anything and every-thing that hurt me. And now, I have a vision, a mission, and a movement to lead. I am always looking for ways to better myself and be someone that others would want to follow. Someone that can lead others into their purpose, their mission, and their vision. Without HBR, none of that would have been possible. It is more than a business strategy program; it is life-changing and soul-nourishing!

ABOUT KORI

Kori is now a three time published Author. She's definitely a dreamer by definition. She sees the glass is refillable, maybe not half full or half empty but with hard work and determination she knows that it can be filled back up when it's empty! She loves her family, blood or chosen and will always encourage them to grow and learn throughout their lives. She believes that with true leadership, we can change the world.

Connect with her at www.korikoch.com/quicklinks

17

AMANDA M'S STORY

I haven't always been a woman of faith; however, once Jesus captured my attention, my life changed. Regardless of where I was in my faith walk, I've lived my life with three intangibles: faith, belief, and hope.

One place where God has my attention is being an adoptive mama. Going through the adoption process was stressful; however, the most stress was felt hearing the multiple layers of trauma within the adoption community. Now that I am a part of it, my own personal traumas were at the forefront as I attempted to put myself in the shoes of the storytellers.

Hearing excerpts of birthmothers' perspectives of surrendering their babies and the plans they made for their children to have better lives than they could provide birthed a compassion I never thought possible. I attempted to put myself in the position of a baby who was familiar with certain sounds—a voice in utero, a certain heartbeat, etc., only to be given to a stranger; this is traumatic in and of itself.

These are situations that aren't shared freely, nor comfortably, to just anyone. To this day, I've learned to set aside my own opinions and dismissive habits for the story that God has brought me to be part of.

By being an adoptive mama, I've had to deal with ignorant and extremely personal questions just because someone is curious, and most often, they were asking questions in front of my child like he wasn't even there.

In situations like that, it's a struggle, and it can be exhausting to avoid getting defensive and choosing to be loving and accepting instead.

Sometimes the asker doesn't realize how offensive they are being by asking, "Where did you get him?" or "How much did it cost to get him?" There are times I'd want to say, "None of your business" or "How would you feel if I asked you that question in front of your kid?", but didn't because I considered it a version of fighting evil with evil. A response I'd give most often was from an educational standpoint such as, "From his first mother" or "He wasn't given up for adoption; a plan was made with careful consideration," yet those can be a mouthful.

Generally, adoptive parents take training on how to handle criticism and judgements by role-playing in groups, reading about it in books and resources. However, it's a different ballgame entirely when you are out in public.

Now, imagine being a multi-cultural family like we are. It can be brutal being scoffed at or accused of stealing a child of their kind.

There was a long period of time when I sat and wondered, "How can I best educate people?" and thought, "I want to be a safe place for mamas like me." I've even asked, "How am I going to make this happen for you, Lord?"

Lately, it comes out in prayers: "Lord, I feel you pressing on my heart to educate from the place you have me in. How do I go about this without telling someone else's story?" All while training my motherly instincts to remain open to what He has for us as a family.

Ghandi said, "Be the change you want in the world," and I think about it often as a way to teach compassion by showing compassion.

I felt I'm led to write about the struggles and the educational pieces, too. I took a blogging course and started writing the message on my heart; then, my vision got derailed when I was given a bunch of things "to do" first. Once I was ready to go, I was told that my vision wasn't viable.

How frustrating! I felt undermined and super discouraged, especially after spending the money I had for seemingly unimportant gobbledygook only to be buried in information. My gut asked, "Do I really need all this for a blog?" Not to mention, the waste of time already put into it. I was exhausted as it was.

Soon, I threw my hands in the air and determined that, just like everything else in my life, I'd figure it out. Considering everything else I was already "figuring out," the pressure to hold space was mounting.

My role as a transracially adoptive mama in an open adoption is not for the faint of heart. Setting up dates, times, and locations for meetups with multiple kids along with their personal struggles is a big undertaking. When it's time to part ways, it's incredibly difficult, and we are guaranteed to have an emotional hang-over the next day.

Although we have an open adoption, witnessing the emotional struggle my son faces helps me to acknowledge the unacknowledged pain within myself. Helping my son walk through his emotions gives me space to walk through mine in a healthier way.

Would it be "easy" to pass over his experiences and blanket

them with empty and wishful words? Yes. Would it serve him? The answer is no.

For the last few years, I was in an out of working a physically intensive job and sustained an injury that has made me disabled enough to not be able to work certain types of jobs yet not disabled enough for a permanent medical declaration. This kept me in a perpetual state of anxiety where I was constantly juggling between doctors' appointments, physical therapy, and childcare, leaving me very little time to care for myself on a limited disability income.

I was then diagnosed with type 1 diabetes and a congenital condition named mosaic Turner syndrome (MTS). This left me very little choice but to change my personal lifestyle and handle my health. I hit my knees to thank God for the hedge of protection I never knew was there. Considering my MTS went undiagnosed and unmonitored for forty-two years and I've made it this far, I am beyond grateful. I learn new things on a regular basis that need to be addressed to help me thrive, so I can show up and be the best version of myself every day.

A short time ago, I had the opportunity to say good-bye to my dad, who was about to lose his long battle with cancer. It was his dying wish for me to live with no regrets. It meant the world to me to see him once again after years of hardship between us.

It felt like I've had monkey wrench after monkey wrench thrown into my life, and then a struggling marriage was added into the mix. I'm grateful I have my faith in God to rest in. His mighty strength can bear the weight of all of this. I will be relying on Him as my son's life will be rocked again when he learns his father will not be living with us much longer. Even though we are parting ways as amicably as possible, my life as an adoptive single mom with health issues begins very soon. Through all this, I have faith in God that He's got me and all of this, and my true job is to trust Him.

With all this heaviness and periods of waiting, a few things I have done and continue to do to lighten the load are journaling, talk therapy, listening to personal development audiobooks and podcasts while tending my flowerbeds.

Now, I share all of this to say that when life is tough, you are stronger when you lean in on the power of God. My trust in Jesus became stronger through this, and the nudges of the Holy Spirit have become familiar as I learned to navigate my life.

I've been looking for a way to hold space for mamas, and God, in His goodness, led me to a woman who would show me how to do just that.

Enter Martha Krejci.

After being in a group Zoom with her and a team of people I was working with in a network marketing company, the Holy Spirit nudged me to listen to what she had to say. The encouragement that exuded from her told me that she was a good person to get to know.

A few months later, she rolled out her signature program Home-Based Revolution. I didn't bat an eye; I was in! It didn't take long for many more deeply buried hunches and ideas to surface.

Once again, I was able to feel the heart pain of what goes on in the world of adoption and how it needs to be given a voice. For the first time, I had a glimmer of hope of how to share what I had done in all the periods of waiting—through personal struggles, family tension, and so much more, all to show someone how they can get through their struggles, too.

Along the way, Martha connected me with an opportunity to life coach with Oola, and now, balance is being restored.

Thanks to Martha and her willingness to be like Moses, I now have a space with faith-based personal development as a mama and coach who helps other mamas recenter themselves in their messes.

ABOUT AMANDA M.

Amanda Moss is personal development coach and a course creator with a homesteading focus. She is also an adoptive single mom who loves Jesus & finds peace in a garden.

She is passionate about helping moms with a lot on their plate to find balance and take care of themselves. Amanda feels it's important to acknowledge who you are in Christ so you can be present where you are at in the moment. She has loves to encourage personal growth through God's word.

It took her a decade to find a way her voice and want to shorten that time for other mamas however possible. She's on a mission to help as many women as she can to find and lean into the woman God created them to be.

If you are ready to embrace who you are, find balance in your life, show up authentically, and impact the world, then head on over to her website at https://amandamoss.com/links-to-follow-me/, grab her free resources, join her online community, and share space with her.

18

SWATI'S STORY

I was stressed out. Though I was grateful for my family and I loved my profession, the stress of waking up every morning to drop the kids off to school before heading to work and coming home absolutely exhausted was taking its toll on me.

The pandemic gave me a chance to work from home, which meant not rushing to and from work, no school pick-ups, and no more being on my feet for hours at a time. I was thankful for this, but it confused my professional mind. Being a physical therapist with a specialization in manual therapy, I was completely focused on my hands-on skills, patient interaction, and understanding patient psychology. Using my hands to relieve my patients' pain and working in close proximity with them was an everyday deal for me, and I thrived on that interaction with them. But this was no longer an option due to safe distancing rules. I had to tweak my existing knowledge to learn the ropes of virtual (online) consultations.

As if this was not challenging enough with all the technology involved, I also had to carry out other administrative tasks, such as arranging and coordinating in-house trainings and setting up the framework for courses to be held in the future. I had never done anything apart from maybe writing a few blogs. This was a new ball game for me. I felt as though I had to prove my worth in an unrelated field to be employed. I was feeling completely lost.

I was good at my work, but the challenge of working with technology was getting to me. I did not understand how to condense all my hands-on knowledge into a virtual consultation. How was I supposed to work if I did not perform manual therapy on my patients? All these questions that seem trivial today were weighing down heavily on my mind back then and making me feel incompetent. Being a perfectionist who always excelled at any given task, these unfamiliar tasks at work were making me feel inadequate and unskilled.

It was one such day when I was feeling completely pushed into a corner that I literally dropped down to my knees. I was feeling judged for having miserably failed at a business-related task that was definitely not my area of expertise. I decided to just shut down all the negative thoughts in my head and randomly clicked on a video on Facebook so that I could clear my mind. That was the day I discovered Martha Krejci.

Martha was so direct, no fluff and to the point. There was something about her that completely fascinated me. Her style of talking was so casual, and it was easy to relate to her. She wasn't trying to sell me her course, but she gave information for free that one would pay for. I immediately joined her Facebook group and was totally blown away by her. I decided to buy her course on setting up my network marketing business, which I was halfway done with when she released her signature program called HBR.

I had always wanted to have my own practice as a physical

therapist, but there were a million doubts in my head. I did not have the courage to leave the security of a job and put all my eggs in one basket. But Martha was taking it a step further by talking about multiple income streams that included coaching, consulting, and even courses! Even though I was familiar with virtual consultations by now, how could an introvert like me go out there on social media and build a whole business around it?

Despite all the thoughts holding me back, I could feel the taps on my shoulder telling me that HBR was the right way to go. A phrase I had read ages ago kept playing in my head on a non-stop loop every single day—"If you're not building your dreams, you're working towards building someone else's dreams." Another nudge was from my father who has been telling me for years to venture out on my own. My friend lovingly pointed out how I would eagerly learn the ropes of the business world if it was my own business at stake. All these nudges made me decide to take the plunge into Martha's world. Thus started my journey with HBR.

I realized within the first month that HBR was not just about multiple sources of income, it was a complete system that changed a person from the inside out. What I didn't know before taking the plunge into Martha's world was that my mindset was about to expand in an exponential way, not just on a personal but also on a professional level. My confidence level was going to be on rocket boosters.

Before HBR, I always had a voice in the back of my mind telling me that I wasn't good enough with my work. Even though I had the qualifications and skill sets to prove otherwise, I would always doubt myself and compare myself with those around me. I was quite satisfied with my work, but that little niggle of doubt always haunted me. I felt like there was an imposter in my brain, trying to undermine my confidence.

As I listened to Martha and all the experts in the HBR world, I realized that I was pretty good at what I did. My confidence started to build up slowly and gradually. All the introspection I had done during the mindset work made me realize that I wanted to niche down on posture as my specialization. Today, I'm a certified posture expert from American Posture Institute, and I'm able to help my patients better than ever. My job satisfaction has doubled. I sleep at night, thrilled that I actually helped a person change their life that day.

On a personal level, I have been able to pause and analyze my state of mind before I respond to an unpleasant situation. I have learned the art of managing my time better with Martha's tips on time management. That has enabled me to be a better and less stressed out mum.

Another big lesson I learned was to stop judging my worth based on other people's opinion of me. This may sound cliché, but it was something I could only implement once I shifted my mindset and felt more confident about myself.

Today, I feel more relaxed and focused. I have mapped out the next five years of my dream life, and I am gradually working my way towards it. Martha promised me that dream of mine could come true. She showed me the ropes of building my online business with multiple income streams. Today, I'm a certified posture expert with plans to set up my own practice along with courses, virtual consultations, and coaching programs. I could only do so because Martha believed in me, even when I didn't. She brought out all of this hidden potential within me with her blueprint called Home-Based Revolution, and for that, I am eternally grateful.

ABOUT SWATI

Swati is a physical therapist with a special interest in the spine & certified posture expert.

Growing up, she had a poor posture with a slumped back and rounded shoulders. It took her years of persistent practise to transition to a good posture. Today her passion is to help people correct their poor posture and related aches and pains. These can range from heel pain to headaches and everything in between! She guides people to understand their diagnosis & symptom and thus move towards self management of their conditions using simple physiotherapy strategies and easy lifestyle changes.

Connect with her at https://withswati.com/links

19

KARI'S STORY

Where can hopes and dreams be found on the other side of devastating disappointment?

After a series of unfortunate and life-changing events, I woke up one day and didn't recognize my life. It was as if the opposites of all my dreams had come true, and now, I found myself divorced, with no children, without a job, living with my parents, trying to figure out how to survive and pay off astronomical debt. Not surprisingly, depression set in hard and heavy, and the heartache of feeling unworthy, unwanted, and not good enough ran deep. Some days, I could barely get out of bed to take care of my little dachshunds.

As if those bitter heartaches weren't enough, nothing could have prepared me for the overwhelming and unbearable feeling that I was a total and complete failure (not to mention a tremendous disappointment) to my family. After all, I'd always wanted (and planned) to marry and have children. Likewise, I had also fully expected to maintain and rise in my career and anticipated retiring soon, maybe even early? But now, with the crushing weight of these life-altering events, my once lofty goals wilted down to the point that all I really wanted was to just be back out on my own, taking care of my little dogs, independent once more.

While it's shocking how quickly, completely, and dramatically circumstances can change, as the poet Longfellow once said, "Into each life, some rain must fall." Just as suddenly, life can become breathtakingly beautiful and amazing, because even in the darkest depths of despair, God is with us. He has such a perfect, loving way of opening our minds, eyes, and hearts to things forgotten, providing opportunities to lean on others when needed and to unburden ourselves by talking and sharing, instead of keeping emotions and worries bottled up inside.

Finding a quasi-clear pathway through the thick fog of depression and making myself function again was a daunting enough task, but the mere thought of being launched into the wide world of fellow jobseekers made my blood run cold. It had been many years since I'd last looked for employment, and much had changed in that time. Even writing a basic, up-to-date resume was no longer as straightforward as it used to be, but I did it. Still, I was lost, with no true sense of direction. I knew the type of job I had before was not my passion. At that moment, I hit rock-bottom. All I could do was pray for God's divine intervention.

Since there was nothing moving forward on the job search front, I decided to take advantage of this unique opportunity to explore other ideas. Taking time to think about all the possibilities that had caught my interest at one point or another, I felt inspired to take a few classes and work on some certifications in several areas. It was both exciting and encouraging to rekindle my love for learning.

As a result of this new phase of self-discovery, I was further blessed to have the chance to enjoy fellowship with some very special friends who spoke openly on topics at deep, personal levels that I'd never had the opportunity to share with them before.

This is precisely the type of fortuitous conversation I had with a friend who was working hard to grow her own business … and she mentioned a woman named "Martha."

By the time I learned about Martha, I had already decided that striking out on my own had a lot more appeal than going back to the same type of job I'd previously had. I'd revived my lifelong passion for all things related to health and wellness and was determined to see where it could take me. My friend was doing something similar, so we discussed how we might work together and support each other. She told me about a coaching program she was planning to work through and suggested I check it out. She said the coach, Martha Krejci, had been so successful in building a multi-stream income from home that she was amazing everyone.

At the time, I was still trying to figure out exactly what I wanted to do and what it would look like. I needed to sort out how to make a business work.

I decided to spend some time checking out Martha's videos to see if she was the "real deal." I figured that IF she wasn't, I hadn't lost anything but time. But if she was …

I don't recall how many hours I spent watching her videos. I took notes like a mad woman. Good grief! Who was this in-your-face, telling-it-straight entrepreneur with so much energy and passion? It was so refreshing! PLUS, she shared all her information for free; she did it with a godly servant's heart while - at the same time - making an impact. That was some-thing I'd not experienced in my working world, but I instinc-tively knew that I wanted to be a part of that!

But the self-doubt crept back in with a vengeance. Was this, indeed, something *I* could really do? The old tapes of negativity started playing in my head. What if I really didn't have what it took?

Fortunately for me, I was in desperate need of someone to speak to me frankly while simultaneously understanding and encouraging me about all the other possibilities there are in life, and Martha didn't hesitate to remind me that when certain plans come crashing down, there can be (and are) completely different opportunities to be found on the other side. Thank God that she was willing to show me exactly how she accomplished those dreams, with precise steps in building a business, without having to be "sleazy, salesy, and weird" and offering her unwavering support the entire way! That's why I'm all about it!

So I did it! I jumped into the Home-Based Revolution. Immediately, I felt like I was back in college, working on a master's degree in business and marketing, and all I had to start with was poster board and crayons. Neither business nor marketing are my native language, and I had a lot to figure out. Fortunately, everything was laid out step-by-step and so simply that I was blown away.

Fast forward six months, I've experienced some incredible changes. My business is developing and growing in directions I never expected. I'm figuring out multiple income streams that are beginning to help knock out that overwhelming debt. Most importantly, I've been reminded to believe in myself and that it's okay to dream again.

Have I reached my goal of being on my own, taking care of my little dachsies? No, not yet. BUT it's coming! How do I know? Because I'm no longer the sad, depressed, divorced, single female with no dreams. I spent most of my life struggling with feelings of being unworthy and not good enough. I missed out on a lot because those feelings kept me from participating in life. HBR has impacted me the most by helping me discover my own worthiness. I've uncovered a passion I didn't know existed.

Investing in yourself is important when you are struggling to establish goals and find a God-given purpose. Taking time to spend in Bible study, reflection, and prayer was my initial investment. Through that, God led me to connections I needed ... all in His perfect timing. For me, the connections brought me the opportunity to further invest in myself, not only take care of my financial responsibilities, but it also brought a major course in personal growth and development, even when I didn't know I needed it.

Maybe you've dealt with some of the same things I have. Perhaps you're wondering what's on the other side of lost dreams and disappointment. I know the best place to start.

ABOUT KARI

Kari Lyn is a family-centered, dachshund-obsessed entrepreneur with a heart for helping others and serving the Lord. She's a former teacher with a Masters in education turned creative aromatherapist and holistic health advocate. She immerses herself into all things that can support a healthy mind and body, while sharing that knowledge with women struggling to see their dreams beyond excruciating disappointment. Kari's passion is to help women overcome past trauma and heal from the anxiety and depression that can accompany those experiences.

Kari delivers a unique approach to 1:1 Aromatherapy Coaching and is an expert in the relaxation modalities of Raindrop Technique, Vitaflex, and Emotional Release, licensed through C.A.R.E., NCTB, and FSHLB. She strives to inspire others to better understand how their body speaks to them when it needs care, nurturing, and healing.

Connect with Kari Lyn at http://findingkarilyn.com/page/links

20

JILL'S STORY

In 2018, I jumped out of a stable corporate career, and a company I had been with more than half my adult life, to start my own business. I felt so free that day and will never forget the confirmation I received from God just after giving my notice. I had spent ten out of the last eleven and a half years counting down the days when I would leave. I prayed to be one of the people impacted by the infamous Tuesday morning layoffs. I mean, who prays to be laid off? Well, I did, often!

I was ready to live life differently but was far too afraid to make any changes. I started the job based on what I felt I "should" do, and it made sense at the time in my marriage. At about a year and a half in, I wanted to leave, but there was always an excuse. First, it was "my husband would not be okay with it," then it was "when I am fully vested," then "when I have this much in my 401k," then "but they have such great benefits," "I should be responsible," then this, then that ... there was always a reason to stay where I was. But I was miserable. I was literally living in *Groundhog Day* and not in a fun way. Life was just happening to me. I could not believe I was taking time away from my kids to do what I was doing.

Yet, I stayed.

Fast forward to year seven with the company. I had a six-year-old and one-year-old, and I was going through a divorce. Now I stayed because it was stable, and I needed a little stability in my life. Not to mention, I was going to be the only income earner and responsible person in my home. No pressure!

A lot changed in a short amount of time. I was no longer in a marriage that was holding me back, but the job still was. I felt so stuck that I literally thought Bill Murray was going to show up at my door one morning, asking me what day it was.

I was so burnt out. Everything kept going wrong. A month after my ex moved out, the roof leaked for the first time in the fifteen years we lived there. Then, the refrigerator went. I never witnessed so much traffic on my way to and from work. When I got home at night, I barely made it through my kids' dinner and baths and prep for the next day before I would be snoozing on the couch. Each day was about taking care of the kids, working, doing chores … over and over and over. One night that winter, I was snow blowing three feet of snow that fell that afternoon (yes, three feet in just a few hours) when I simultaneously heard my son scream and realized that I could no longer see the four-foot fence surrounding the pool area in my back yard.

At that moment, I burst into tears and laughter at the same time. It was almost midnight, I had to get up with the kids in a few hours; now, I had to stop to console my son, and the snow removal was not even close to done. I shouted out loud, "God, am I being filmed for someone's entertainment? Am I on 'The Truman Show'?"

It still took me a little bit, but I finally surrendered. I chose this life. I was the one doing it all without asking for help. I was the one living in this house that is more than I would like to handle. I was the one staying at a job I hate. I was the one that was living for everyone else but myself. These were all choices I was making. I was stressed, overwhelmed, and burnt out.

I was not providing the life I desired for my kids to have. They did not deserve a stressed-out mom who worked all the time and had little patience. They deserved more, and I had to find a way to give it to them.

In hindsight, yes, I deserved that amazing life too, but I was not quite at the point of admitting that I actually wanted an amazing life. I did not feel I deserved it. My motivation was my kids and my dog. I did admit that day that my life was full of choices, and it was time I made choices towards a more fulfilling life for them.

So I sought out a coach and jumped into "what do I need to fix in me to make a better life for my kids?" mode. I read the books. I asked the questions. I did the work. And after a little while, I realized that in order for my kids to have a life that dreams are made of, I must be the example, and I must pursue the life I dream of. I did not know yet what I desired for my life, but I was going to figure it out.

I dove deep into my own healing, spending countless hours transforming myself mentally, emotionally, physically, and, most of all, spiritually. It took quite some time, but it was worth every second. I finally rediscovered who I was. I began to trust myself again. I bonded even deeper with my kids. I was being the mom I desired to be for them. I connected with my purpose. I began to shine my light again. Groundhog Day was now only one day a year, on February 2nd, when Punxsutawney Phil reveals his prediction for the start of spring. I was no longer living it over and over again.

Then, one day, on my drive from work to see my life coach, I felt a nudge. Why was I going to work each day for someone else at a job that did not light me up when I could do something else?

I followed that nudge and was inspired to leap into entrepreneurship just a few weeks later without a plan. Entrepreneurship was a missing piece for many reasons. I am able to express my creativity, inspire others, and prioritize my and my children's relationship and well-being to name a few. I am passionate about helping other mom's escape their *Groundhog Day* life and create a life they love for and with their children.

And now, I leap more often because I trust myself to follow where my energy pulls me. Do not get me wrong, I do not recommend anyone just jump out of their job without a plan; however, taking a leap towards a dream is so much better than staying stagnant in a lackluster life. Right? Trust yourself. Trust God. Trust the universe. Trust the nudges you get. Trust. And ACT on that trust.

I was mindlessly scrolling Facebook late one Sunday evening, exhausted from a busy week of doing "all the things" and feeling like I had not gotten anywhere.

While winding down with a meditation may have been a better way to prepare for sleep, I found myself scrolling that night. The universe brought this woman to me who, unbeknownst to me at the time, would change my and my kids' lives for the better.

Trusting my gut was not new to me anymore. When I felt a nudge, I went with it, even when it did not always seem to make the most sense. The energy I felt that night from her video was similar to an energy I felt a couple years before when I made one of the biggest leaps of my life. I trusted the nudge I felt on that Sunday night Facebook scroll, and I messaged the words "Case Study" to the business strategist who got me dreaming that my little business could truly be an empire one day. The amazing Martha Krejci is helping me to gain clarity, confidence, calm, systems, and processes in my business, and in life, for that matter.

I am creating a legacy for my kids with them by my side. I am thinking about and implementing things into my life that I never dreamt of before. I am a published author (more than once) for goodness sake! I have a book series outlined, and the kids and I have a children's book planned. My Reiki business is expanding. I launched a coaching program. I am creating journals, swag, and other fun things. Most of all, I am a model to my kids to pursue what they are passionate about and that no matter your circumstances, your age, or the place you are in life, you can dream and pursue what fills you up. My kids are coming to me with book ideas, product ideas, things they could do and sell, and so many ways they can serve our community.

We are shining our lights brighter, and we are lifting those around us. I choose me. I choose my kids. I choose to dream and to go after those dreams. For the first time, I can confidently say, "Watch out world; here we come!" and mean it in a positive, build-an-empire kind of way.

Please remember, wherever you are in life, there is always hope. Your energy affects everyone and everything around you. Feed your energy with positivity and love. Seek what lights you up and find a community that will support you as you are and challenge you to get where you are going. Put yourself first, bring in your kids, and impact the world.

Namaste.

ABOUT JILL

Jill is a Multidimensional Energy Healer & Teacher, Life Coach, Content Creator, Published Author & High Vibe Spiritual Mama.

She inspires moms who feel stuck in Groundhog day to shift their energy and live differently. She empowers them to prioritize their self-care & spirituality, stop "shoulding" on themselves and rewrite their stories in order to create a life and legacy they love for and with their kids.

Her mama motto is "Mama first, bring in the kids, impact the world!"

Jill's personal healing journey inspired her to make changes in her life that have helped her and her family find more love, joy & abundance. The impact of this was so great that she left her corporate career to start her own business focused on helping families heal too.

When we heal and take care of ourselves, we heal the world around us. Let's shift the energy of this world together! Are you ready?

Connect with Jill at https://jillcoletti.com/links

21

ERICA'S STORY

After ten years of striving and planning, praying and begging, all my dreams had

come true. I married the man of my dreams, beat incredible less than one percent odds of conceiving, and went through a whirlwind of infertility and secondary infertility. The result was four beautiful boys and two angel babies, and my dream of being a SAHM had come true. Done birthing babies, the process of pouring myself out becoming a mother and motherhood stripped me of all but a few threads of my identity, including the ability to create any new dreams.

There were a few things growing up that I knew that I wanted in my future. One was to be a mother, and the other was to be an entrepreneur. I also wanted to do "the right" things that would give me success in my life. Everyone said college was "the golden ticket" to the life I wanted. No one in my family had ever attended college, and most didn't finish high school. Even though I grew up in the shadow of a big ten university, college was never talked about, and I really didn't understand what it was. Through my entire childhood, the message was made clear through movies and media. Go to college, get a good job, and start a family. I was one hundred percent sold that was the way to a happy life. So that was my plan. In order to accomplish this goal, I worked two jobs to avoid taking out student loans and took a full course load. Degree earned. Goal reached. Now what?

Most of my first jobs after college utilized the skills I learned earning my minor in communications. I paid the bills with various types of advertising jobs, but it wasn't until I got my first taste of freedom in a sales position that I remembered my dream of being an entrepreneur. It would be several years before I would begin to chase the entrepreneur dream again with several try / fail attempts.

Around the time my youngest son was two, I knew that I wanted to build a business to contribute to the family's finances and give me something "of my own" to be proud of. I chose an MLM company whose products I was in LOVE with and set off on my journey to help others and, in the process, create wealth and financial independence while sharing products I loved. Or so I thought ... I DID love the products. I DID love telling people about them. So what was wrong?

Don't get me wrong, I had some measure of success, *more than most* but not as much as others. But I had never worked so hard for something month after month with no feeling of reward. I had passion but no purpose. For the first time in my life, no amount of work ethic got me the desired outcome. Worse, I had developed a terrible cycle of self judgement and punishment, shame and blame for what I considered repeat failures. The community I sought turned out to be, with a few exceptions, like high school all over again, mean girl cliques and all. After four years of working heart and soul, I felt defeated and hopeless. I still wanted to make a difference in people's lives; I still needed to contribute to my family. I asked myself "would my entrepreneur dreams ever come true?"

Around the same time, I was falling out of love with my network marketing company. I began following a business strategist, and everything she talked about resonated with me. "Would this be just another training?" I asked myself. I warily stalked Martha Krejci on Facebook for months, wondering if she really was as different as she claimed to be. However, I noticed that I was excited about what she had to say regarding how I could show up authentically and help people.

A few months after dipping a toe into one of her programs, she unveiled the Home-Based Revolution (HBR). I almost didn't do it. I honestly didn't believe enough in myself at the time to justify the investment. I wanted to believe I could do it, and I knew that in all the training that Martha had ever provided, she *over delivered*. I tentatively asked my husband if he thought I should/could do it. Would he support me? He agreed. In hindsight, he's always been my biggest cheerleader. He always wants to see me succeed. I remember hitting send and literally shaking. It was the most money at one time I ever invested in my personal development.

It didn't take me long to identify who I wanted to serve from my heart. I knew right away that I wanted to help other couples who had been told that they weren't candidates for IUI/IVF, that they couldn't be helped with traditional interventions. I wanted them to know that just because a doctor told them that **he/she** couldn't help them didn't mean that they couldn't get pregnant. I wanted them to know that I didn't get pregnant because I was special but because I was willing to exhaust any and all obstacles to get to the family of our dreams.

Thanks to my leap of faith into HBR, my college degree has

not been wasted. Every skill I learned from my degree and job experience has been unlocked in HBR. When I look back at the last year, I can distinctly remember how I felt, what my goals were, and what dreams I had. I can tell you that inside, I feel like that was at least three times as long ago as the one year it has been. Many of my best friends have joined me in HBR, and I've developed my abilities to encourage them, helping them see in *themselves* what I see in *them*.

To see your friends serving in their purpose and impacting the world in a huge way is such an amazing blessing. Now, I don't just dream of how I can impact individual families dealing with infertility, but I'm determined to change the reproductive medical system by putting the power in the patient's hands through empowerment and education.

My self-talk has changed over the course of the past year, and I'm relearning how to manage my inner dialog and not allow negative thought patterns to control my life. Buried deep in my heart, I have uncovered generational goals of being a published author, and this year, I'll fulfill that, not once but twice. Slowly, I am taking back my power and dreaming dreams again. I no longer feel the need to grind myself into dust to prove my effort is "enough." I've become open to all possible ways to serve other women struggling, and now, that includes being a postpartum doula.

Over the course of this year and my "business training," I have healed so many wounds that I was still hiding from myself. It has shown me that my value isn't tied to my performance, it's okay to try and fail and try again, and perfection is a myth. I have found the community of women that I've longed for, and although I still have a difficult time asking them for help, I know that they're there for me.

I can't imagine a fiercer group of women on the planet than

women who go through infertility. When you are faced with being stripped of your dreams and what society deems to be an essential component of what makes you a woman, you have a different perspective when your dream of motherhood is fulfilled. I know there is a whole group of women out there that I can help get on the path to the baby of their dreams but also fiercely fight for the life of THEIR choosing. After all, beating the odds of *making a baby* are MUCH bigger than beating the odds of *making the life of your dreams*. When your turn comes, don't let the opportunity pass you by. Fight for the life your dreams.

ABOUT ERICA

Erica Hoke is the infertile mother of four boys, all born to her as a "geriatric" pregnant lady. After struggling for years with undiagnosed endometriosis, uterine fibroids, PCOS, thyroid disease, factor 5 Leiden and MTHFR, unable to participate in traditional IUI or IVF methods, she was able to get to the bottom of her infertility issues via continual changes to her diet and lifestyle.

Now she fiercely shares her story and the stories of others as a means to give hope to those still on the path to creating the family of their dreams. Dissatisfied with the way reproductive endocrinology (REI) medicine handles common infertility issues, Erica is determined to disrupt the entire reproductive medical system. Empowering infertility patients by creating a standard of care and testing path through which to collaborate and coordinate with their doctors has become her mission. This approach allows the patients to systematically address and remove all obstacles before pursuing invasive and expensive IUI and IVF treatments.

Erica mentors clients through the infertility process via a free support group, group coaching, courses to address diet, toxins and lifestyle that affect infertility, and one on one coaching. Struggling with infertility or know someone who is?

Start here: https://ericahoke.com/links

2 2

JANINE'S STORY

Here I go again.

Another day.

Another day of clocking into the same time clock at work after rushing to get there on time.

Another day of rushing to get the kids fed and ready, getting them off to school, then rushing to work, so I would not be late, then putting in a full day of physical work in the healthcare field. After my long day, I have to rush back home to get the kids, then start to make dinner. By that time, with not much left to the day, I am able to see my family. Finally, we get the kids ready for bed. Then, we go to bed. Exhausted.

It was the same thing every. single. day.

I was exhausted. I was exhausted trying to make everything work. I was exhausted waking up very early to get myself ready and to start the daily grind. I was exhausted from being on my feet all day. I was exhausted having to rush home and get the evening ready. I was exhausted doing ALL the work while someone else was getting all the benefits. I was exhausted running on someone else's schedule and time.

And do you want to know what else?

I was exhausted from not receiving any kind of acknowledgement or recognition for a job well done.

I was exhausted from not having time for my family or time for ME! Not only did I feel exhausted, I was also broken. I was broken because after all the hard work I had put into my job, my career, this could not be it. This could not be the rest of my life.

I was in an emotional conflict. I had worked so hard to complete my studies and then have a job in healthcare. Don't get me wrong, I knew I was meant to help people. It is in my blood. I was exhausted and broken in every sense. I was exhausted, physically, emotionally, and spiritually. I even felt distant with God. My exhaustion was also affecting, most importantly, my family life.

I knew this exhaustion was consuming me. I did not know what to do or where to turn. I was stuck. I felt defeated. Then I started wondering, is this it for me? Is this how I am going to spend the next twenty-plus years of my life? Am I going to be doing this rat race, over and over? This is not what I signed up for. THIS is not in my blood.

What was I going to do? I was already working another job, but I did not want to do that either. I knew by me working another job, it was helping my family financially. But it was exhausting me even more.

One day, about a year and half ago, I was going through my normal day-to-day routine. I was clocking in at work, and I saw that my time punch went through. I just stared at the time clock. I kept staring at it, like I was paralyzed. I saw my children's lives flash in front of me. I saw them as babies and fast forward to adults right before my eyes. All I was doing was staring at the time clock. The same time clock. I had to run to the bathroom because I became upset and did not want my co-workers to see me this way.

During this time, I became part of a network marketing company. I loved the products so much that I wanted to share them with everyone I knew. There was an added bonus; I was able to receive an extra paycheck by sharing! Through this network marketing company, I met Martha Krejci. Martha was part of some of the same groups as I was. Martha would do live calls in the groups that we were in.

At first, I just thought she was another one of our leaders in the company. But then, I saw that in just a short period of time, she achieved a rank that normally takes the average person a few years to achieve!

That caught my attention.

I started to pay attention to Martha and her live chats. If I could not make her live chats, I made sure to listen to the replay. She was resonating with me.

Martha is a business strategist. She was sharing her knowledge to those of us who were ready to hear it. And I was ready. I was ready for the revolution!

Martha created a plan called Home-Based Revolution (HBR). This, too, caught my attention. HBR is a very strategic plan to guide individuals to their full potential. This strategic plan provides a step-by-step guide to discover my hidden talents. Yes, talents. HBR guides you on how to develop these talents and present them to your community.

When I heard about HBR, I knew this was for me. I felt it in my heart and soul. When I heard Martha speak about HBR, I knew this was bringing me to the next chapter in my life.

The HBR community is amazing! It is filled with like-minded individuals that want the same thing as me. We all want to know "what else can we do?" "How else can I serve those that need me?"

Besides the amazing community, HBR has changed my mindset. I was someone who always thought there was only one way. Holy cow, was I wrong! First, the mindset work has completely shifted the way I think, the way I feel, and the way I approach life. I have gained so much confidence in myself and my talents that I am not afraid to share them.

Through this program, not only have I discovered myself, but I have developed amazing friendships along the way. Even though we all come from different walks of life, we are there for each other through this amazing journey!

This journey is one that I have never experienced before. I went from thinking that my life was just one road, but now, I have all these opportunities to serve my community. I am not perfect, and neither is my journey, but it is developing, growing, and becoming something beautiful!

And do you know what else?

This is MY journey to MY freedom that no one else can take from me. For the first time, I have hope and a sense of calmness. By discovering myself and how I can serve others, I know that in the future, I will not be doing the daily nine to five grind. I will not be rushing to get everyone ready, rushing to make it to work on time, and not spending enough time with my children. I know that I will not be missing my children's school functions because I have to be at work. This self-discovery has brought peace within me.

I am so excited for these changes that are happening every day. I am excited to see how my path is growing and evolving. I am loving how I am evolving as a leader, as an individual, as a mother, as a wife, as me.

I am on this journey ... are you?

ABOUT JANINE

Janine is living her dream life with her husband of 13 years and 2 beautiful daughters. Janine is a Doctor of Physical Therapy and has an MBA in Health Systems Management. As a health care professional, Janine has always guided others to help heal their bodies.

Janine is also an autoimmune warrior. She was diagnosed with an autoimmune disease, and has been living with it, for over 20 years. Through this journey, she has been through the ebbs and flows of this diagnosis. This journey has driven Janine to help others in a different way. Janine now guides others, with autoimmune disease, to get back into fitness and a healthier eating lifestyle, specifically for autoimmune disease. Janine is also a certified Aroma Freedom Technique Practitioner. She incorporates this technique to guide others through their emotional blockages, so they can achieve their highest potential.

Since Janine was diagnosed with autoimmune disease, it took her 20+ years and many medical appointments, to recognize that she was not receiving the help or advice that she was looking for. Janine is now on a mission to help women with autoimmune disease achieve their health goals.

If you are ready to transform your health and achieve your highest potential, then connect with her at https://bit.ly/3uxYzNj

23

NATALIE'S STORY

It's hard to believe how much my life has changed in just over a year. There have been a lot of outside changes, like job, location, number of children. But the bigger, more important changes have been on the inside. I've struggled with anxiety and shame for most of my life, since I lost my mom at the young age of fourteen. A few years ago, I started to heal from the grief of losing my mom, but I still struggled with belief in myself and still had bouts of anxiety and hopelessness from time to time.

For years, I dreamed of having my own business, working from home, being an author. I even joined multiple MLMs to try and achieve these dreams. But every single time, I let my fear and lack of belief stop me in my tracks. I also dreamed of being a stay-at-home mom, watching my baby grow up, homeschooling. But the reality is that, like most families in the U.S., this seemed impossible to live off a single income. So I did what most of the other moms I knew were doing. I had my son, stayed home with him for twelve weeks, and then headed back to work while someone else got to spend all those precious moments with my babe. The more time that passed, the less I believed that things could ever be different.

I can distinctly remember one afternoon, going for my daily walk in the parking lot of my job on my break, holding back tears and thinking to myself, if this is as good as life gets, what's the point of even staying alive? It's hard to admit that, especially because in my head, I knew how blessed I was. I had a decent job, a wonderful husband, and an amazing son whom I adore. But that's the thing about anxiety, it doesn't always make logical sense. In the moment, all you know is that overwhelming feeling of dread, and all you want is to find a way to escape that feeling. Fortunately for myself and my family, shortly after this incident, a dear friend shared with me about a new mentor she was learning from. We had similar visions for the future of our families, and while I wasn't working the same business as she was, she knew that this system could work for me, too. And she believed in me and my future when my belief was still waning. I honestly wasn't even sure this would work for me, but I liked what I heard and started to have a tiny spark of hope again; plus, the guarantee was pretty sweet, so I figured it was worth giving it a try.

Now, my story is a little different than some of the others here, in that I haven't made a dime since starting HBR. And I don't feel discouraged by that at all. It's not that I haven't helped others; I certainly have. But the help that I've given, in the way of coaching, I haven't charged for until now. At first, I struggled to actually implement what I learned in the course and decided that I would take it at my own pace. Then, I got pregnant and had a tough pregnancy, so I took several months to step back and focus on my family and my health in addition to my full-time job. And now, with newborn in tow, the time has come to really step into my power and change lives, while changing my family's legacy at the same time.

What I want to talk about here, though, is how much my mindset has changed. Like I said, I struggled with believing in myself and believing that I could have a future of my own design. I knew I wanted it, but I had trouble believing that it could actually happen for me. Until I met Martha Krejci. Then, little by little, things started to shift, and I started learning how to believe in myself and trust my worth. I started implementing tools that are taught in HBR in all areas of my life. Instead of giving up on our fertility journey after almost a year and a half of trying to get pregnant, I started saying affirmations and sought assistance through alternative medicine, which resulted in getting pregnant in just five weeks. Instead of continuing to stay in a job with very little opportunity for growth, we decided to finally act on our desire to move to Georgia, and we made that happen.

Instead of settling for putting my kids in daycare and after-care programs while I worked full-time, like I'd always done, we found ways to shift our finances and make staying at home a reality once we moved. Instead of continuing to push pause on my dream of becoming a published author, I took the leap and jumped into a book collaboration and had the short version of my story published in a beautiful book called *The Truth About Success* in April 2021. And now, I'm in a second collaboration and currently working on my own full-length book.

Instead of allowing someone else to teach my son all the things that I always thought I would get to teach him, we made the choice to pull him out of traditional school, sifted through tons of different curriculum choices, chose the ones we felt would work best for our family, and started homeschooling our eight-year-old. There is no doubt in my mind that these things would not have happened if I hadn't taken a leap of faith and jumped in to HBR when I did. The choice is yours, my friend. You can stay where you are, stuck in a place that probably feels mediocre at best, or you can take a chance on a huge opportunity with an incredible guarantee and change the lives of yourself, your family, and those you don't even know yet.

ABOUT NATALIE

Natalie is a wife, mom to two incredible boys, and transformation coach. After losing her own mother at the age of 14, she struggled through 20 years of anxiety, depression, and suicidal thoughts before ultimately finding the right combination of tools to work through her grief and shame. Now she helps others in similar situations to identify their own root issues that are holding them back and sabotaging their lives, in order to process their grief, forgive, and experience a life of hope and freedom. She currently runs a Facebook support group and offers 1:1 coaching sessions, and also has a podcast and book in the works.

Connect with her at: https://findnatalie.com

24

JALEEN'S STORY

The month before I joined HBR, my mom had just had another stroke. She'd had a series of "minor" strokes over the past couple of years that were puzzling, to say the least. Every day, I expected to get a call that she was in the hospital, which would have been a nightmare for me.

I do energetic/intuitive work, so I'm always testing everything to get to the bottom of things and energetically flip the situation for the better. I'd been trying to figure out what was really going on with my mom and why she kept having stroke after stroke, and I finally received a new truth that she was experiencing carbon monoxide poisoning. That really freaked me out. I mean, you can die from that. I told my son, who was her living companion, and he got the house tested for potential carbon monoxide levels. They were off the charts. We immediately evacuated my mom and had her and my son move in with us.

This may sound like an ideal situation to some, to gather those you love together under one roof. But the truth is that my mom and I don't always see eye to eye. Growing up with her as a mom had many ups and downs. She says now that she should never have been allowed to raise children. She simply wasn't designed for that. And while things were not always bad, let's just say there were scary moments. I love my son dearly. Unfortunately, he's a lot like me, so our relationship has not always been the smoothest.

I was already struggling to implement the strategies in an expensive mastermind I'd joined. Strategies that were, if I'm being completely honest, questionable in my mind. And now, with the added workload of caring for my mom and the extra housework, I just didn't have time to even try to make it work. To top it off, my mom wasn't the easiest person to get along with in the first place, and losing her eyesight in the last stroke made things even more difficult. Not only was she miserable, but now she felt useless as well.

Sobbing my heart out as I tumbled into bed late each night, I asked God, "Is this all I'm made for? Is this really what I'm supposed to be doing with my life?" I was so exhausted from all the extra work that I gave up on the expensive mastermind with all its complicated and expensive parts.

My daughter was worn out, too. She's my strong right arm. But this was just too much for both of us to handle. Something had to change. So I quit what I'd been working on. At least for now.

I almost never watch YouTube, but for some reason, I ended up there that day. And there was Martha Krejci, speaking straight to my heart. I don't even remember what she was talking about, but it totally inspired me to look at HBR. Normally, when I make a major financial decision, I pray about it, discuss it with my husband, and sleep on it, before acting. But this was different. The pull to jump in was so strong, I just took a chance and did it. And I have never regretted that choice.

As with any business program, it's easy to get overwhelmed if you try to go too fast. Yes, I'm guilty. I did that. But the saving grace, and what I've gotten the most out of HBR so far, was the personal growth and development tools. I've spent more time with that part than anything else so far, and it's saving my life.

As a result, I'm calm again. I'm taking better care of myself; my home is running much more harmoniously. I'm finally getting clearer on my purpose and who I'm meant to serve. It feels so much better than the direction I was trying to go in the previous program I was in. I feel like I'm shifting from what other "experts" told me I should do—and was frankly a huge struggle—to what I *am* meant to do. I also have a book in the works, which is a huge surprise. I never imagined I'd ever write a book before joining HBR.

Our household finances have improved tremendously. We were living paycheck to paycheck before, but now, we've got nine months' worth of expenses saved and no credit card debt. Being in an ethically-operated program that doesn't expect me to keep forking over thousands of dollars all the time to learn my next step has made a huge difference.

My twenty-six-year-old daughter, who always professed she couldn't write, has published her first book and is working on five more in the same series. She's also hired a team to produce the audiobook version, something none of us imagined.

My thirty-six-year-old son, who had hydrocephalus as a baby and was not expected to live past his thirtieth birthday, is about to receive a million-dollar investment into his start up that he's been working on for the last fifteen months.

Our twenty-nine-year-old son, who's been on the spectrum through most of his life, is a highly sensitive person, and who barely spoke for the last thirteen years, has begun speaking more and more lately. He's also begun creating income streams for himself at last.

My wonderful husband, who's always been super supportive of me and our children, seems happier and more fulfilled. He looks younger, too. Probably because he's not so stressed by the messes the rest of us were experiencing.

Since living with us for the last seven months, six of which I've been in HBR, my mom has shed eighty pounds and says she can't even remember the last time she weighed so little. She's regained the sight in one of her eyes, and the other, which didn't even open when she moved in, now opens freely in sync with her other eye. She hasn't had a single stroke since she moved in. Praise God! She's getting around better and better every day and contributes to the household operations more often, which blesses me so much.

She's also not in pain anymore either, which we figured out was actually emotional pain trapped in her body. Doing the emotional release work that I learned through HBR has been the solution. We are getting along better than we ever have in my fifty-eight years on the planet. And you can't put a price tag on that.

This also reminds me that I haven't had a headache in quite a while. And this was a never-ending problem before HBR.

I am looking forward to implementing more of the HBR strategies. I haven't even begun to grow my business yet. I know that when I do, I will do it by showing up in service to the people I was created to serve. And I know that with Martha and HBR on my side, the sky's the limit!

ABOUT JALEEN

Jaleen is a believer, wife, intuitive & trained healer, business consultant to other healers, and an organizing savant - they call her the "Tetris Queen".

She's also the creator of Life Enhancement Energetics, a system that lets you release the underlying causes of your struggles, so everything flows better in your life.

She's been called Wonder Woman, an Angel, the Queen of Calm, and the Voice of Reason.

When she's not helping other healers let their light shine brighter by creating businesses they love, she's in the kitchen creating delicious raw vegan treats, enjoying inspiring movies with her awesome husband of 37 years, riding her bike around the lake with her sweet daughter, singing uplifting songs at the top of her voice, and choosing to look for the joy in every situation.

Jaleen believes every wholistic wellness woman should have a thriving business that helps heal the world. If that sounds like you, connect with Jaleen at findjaleen.com

"Together we can make Wholistic Wellness the Norm,
NOT the alternative."

25

AMY'S STORY

"This will be it! This will be the one that will finally get us going; I'm sure of it." I must have repeated a chain of similar words more times than I care to remember. This was the phrase I used when I was trying to convince my husband, Shane, to just let me spend a tiny bit more on a training program or advertising adventure that I was sure would take our little family business to the next level. His father had just sent him the biggest blow of his life, and I was desperately trying to make our at home dehydrated food mix business work. Little did I know that only 6 months later, my life would be completely turned upside down.

We had just gotten out of the military and were trying to adjust to our recent loss of income. I was so excited to have the opportunity to stay at home after being frequently deployed as a USAF pilot. For the previous six years, I had missed all of my children's milestones. I was so disconnected from my husband and children, I often felt like a stranger living in my own home. I could finally allow myself to attach to my life, mentally and emotionally.

During out last military relocation, this time from Kansas to California, my youngest son, eight years old at the time, attempted to take his life. He locked himself in an upstairs bedroom and tried to jump out a two-story window into the boulders below. We were able to break down his bedroom door before he was successful. He was upset that the crease on his socks was not in the right place; how could I have missed that my own child was so mentally distraught? I entered a state of darkness. That darkness became even thicker as I sat across from a psychologist who had just evaluated my son. He told me that due to my constant coming and going, my son had developed a type of PTSD. In my son's mind, I had died; he no longer allowed himself to connect with me in order to avoid the pain of repeated separation.

I was done, unable to cope. The military would not release me for a hardship. They pushed me to claim that I was mentally unfit for duty, and I was told that was the only way I could get out. I found an alternate route through my senator, pushed my case to the Pentagon, and, finally, was able to be released from active duty into a guard unit, which placed us back on the Utah/Idaho border, where we both grew up. Things went well for about a year. I was home more, and the business was doing well, but we were still struggling through the past muck of debt from business ideas that did not work. It still seemed like we were just "almost" there, "almost" to a place where we felt like it would really take off. I was always joining the next best "coaching" program, "business building" workshop. They were all the same; nothing really pivoted us into the right location.

Adjusting back into civilian life was proving to be a struggle. Shane was dealing with additional issues with his parents. That has been ongoing throughout our marriage, but this time, it was really hitting him hard. The front view of our new house looks right into the back of his parents' business, the one he had been promised he would have the opportunity to take over. His dad gave the keys to Shane's uncle instead, and Shane was emotionally traumatized.

Our marriage was falling apart; financial stressors and the constant "dumping" of money into a business that was not stable was taking its toll. One day, Shane left the house, and he never came back. He ended up giving in to the dark waters of depression and lost his life to suicide.

I tried to pick up the pieces; on the outside, I looked strong, like a warrior. Amy is a survivor, a fighter, she is always successful. I tried to keep my business going, but without Shane, it was draining me. Lost and broken, I fell into a narcissistic marriage with another widow. Both of us had past unhealed trauma and were in a relationship feeding on complete chaos. I wanted to end my life, give up. I felt so lost, like I had nothing left to give. The once "pilot on a pedestal" with a clear view of her mission had died inside. I was being controlled by my spouse from the moment I woke up to the moment I fell asleep. I no longer had any connections to family or friends.

I got pregnant. It was a small little ray of sunshine on my cloud-covered life. We were adding a girl to our family of all boys. My marriage was still a complete mess, and by that point, I had sold my business and taken on a corporate job. My children were the only anchor I had, the only thing that kept my head above water.

We found out that our daughter had a heart defect at our twenty-week ultrasound. "Oh God, how can this be happening? I can't do it!" I heard encouraging words around me, "You have been through so much; everything will be fine." I learned to hate that phrase. Everything is not always fine; baby sister passed away twenty-six days after she was born.

I struggled with my mental health for a year. I had to make a choice, give up or change. I chose to change. My life has been too difficult to not have a purpose! I began working on myself, and I gave my husband an ultimatum to get on board or get out. Slowly, the storm began to lift, and I found myself in the world of energy work. Everything started to make sense, how I have felt my whole life, the damage from my childhood, my ability to "sense" things and understand people on a deeper level. This is a divine gift, not a burden. I began to emerge from my cocoon; with wet wings, I started to reach for my potential.

My passion was burning; my soul was on fire! My business gave purpose to my life, the loss of Shane, the passing of baby sister. I have learned to develop this skill; I can reach out to my daughter at any time, and I want this beautiful gift to be something that everyone experiences. A full body, mind, soul balance and Elevate Life Vibration is born. My past traumas, the dark spots on my soul, scars that continually break open, have now turned into a beautiful purpose. I am blessed as I work with clients, bursting with gratitude as I see their joy return, their pain literally disappear, and they see things like their nonfunctional thyroid return to a balanced state. Their life starts to become a magnet for abundance, and things that weighed them down dissolve and are replaced with things they only thought they could imagine!

I loved my corporate job and was able to keep some balance in my life. I came across a client who led me to Martha Krejci, and with some resistance, I checked out her page and started watching her. This lady is fire. I am so aligned with her spark. But I have been here before, spending money on the next "best" coaching platform. My mind goes back to Shane and the financial mess that led him into darkness. I reached out to Martha anyway; she messaged me back. I didn't have the finances to join her tribe, but I knew it was right. The universes align, and after a couple of conversations, I find a way to make it work.

I log in, expecting for it to be another "no brainer" why did I pay for this information? Instead, it's gold, pure liquid gold. After literally only spending an hour watching, I had a notebook full of ideas! I began to add them to my day, and my business takes off! I began to not only work on clients for their own issues, I began a course to teach others how to do this work on themselves and others. The number of lives I can touch has become infinite!

So there I sat, at my corporate job, thinking about how this has all unfolded for me. A voice pops into my head, "This job is costing you money." My ego kicks in and starts to argue with my higher-level consciousness. You're making your ideal salary, you have benefits, and this is just like when you tried this before; you left the military, it cost you Shane, devastated you to your hands and knees.

I heard myself reply, "The only thing that will stop my success is YOU." I cleared the self-doubt, I walked down to my boss's office, and I quit my job. I never looked back. Life is about the "now," in this moment, what can you do right now. You don't look at the past; you release the fear of the future, and the more you align yourself with your true purpose, your vibration raises, and the more higher vibrating things are attracted to you. The possibilities are endless!

ABOUT AMY

Amy is a true example of how life can give you everything, then take it all way! Amy was an aspiring military pilot who thought she had it all until her husband lost his life to suicide. She was left a single mom to her ten- and thirteen-year-old boys. Amy later remarried and then lost her only daughter to a heart defect.

Amy completely fell down the rabbit hole, she had lost all hope, self-confidence and any spark from her previous accomplishments had smoldered way. With divine intervention she was led into the world of energy healing. After fulling embracing the beautiful practice of releasing past traumas, Amy went on to develop her own methodology for trauma recovery and Elevate Life Vibration was born.

Amy now uses her past as her purpose, fulfilling her passion by bringing joy and smiles back to those who have been burdened by physical, mental or emotional obstacles.

Connect with her at https://linktr.ee/honestsassymama

26

AMANDA'S STORY

Call me weird; really, it's okay. I have always loved supporting a mom through her childbirth experience. I was blessed to be with my sister and my ex-sister-in-law when they had their babies more than twenty years ago, and those were such exciting experiences. Then, I had my first baby, and the desire to support women through their pregnancy and childbirth journeys grew stronger. After having my first homebirth, that calling was stronger than ever.

Childbirth is such a primally beautiful display of the strength, determination, perseverance, and sheer willpower that women hold within their bodies. Some women are never given the chance to feel that power, and that makes me sad for them. I want to change this through sharing my story, what I have learned, and the stories of other women who have experienced amazing and empowered births.

A few years ago, in a random conversation, a couple told me that I needed to have an outlet, like YouTube, where I could share the information I had been sharing with them. I was enthralled with the idea and went home excited to run with it. It lit me up to think about sharing the knowledge I had from my own experiences and from other women who had also had widely different experiences as well.

I could talk about pregnancy and childbirth all day long!

I never really thought about this idea possibly becoming an income stream, although I guess I thought that if I could get seen enough, I would start making money with it somehow. That wasn't important to me at the time; I just wanted to serve women on their own beautiful journeys in having amazing experiences.

I was pregnant with my fourth child at the time, and eventually, the idea got moved to the back burner and life moved on. I still talked about pregnancy and childbirth any chance I got, and of course, I shared with anyone who asked that I would be having our baby at home again.

Then, in the spring of 2020, a friend recommended a course called Go for Gold for building a network marketing business that we were both in. I jumped in, started working my way through the course, and loved what Martha stood for and how she was teaching people to build heart-centered, servant-minded businesses authentically.

When she launched her signature course, Home-Based Revolution (HBR), I jumped in and started to really dig in to who I wanted to serve and how.

Where could I serve all day long and not get tired of it? Pregnancy and childbirth!

I was so excited to be getting back to that idea from back in 2018. As I went through her course, I began to see exactly how I could take that idea and fit it right in to the system she was teaching. I had my passion back and was again on fire to get this idea up and going. This time, the vision was so much bigger and had far more impact with the things I was about to learn.

HBR took my passion and asked me to dig deeper still. Who did I want to serve? How did I want to serve them? Where could I draw from that fulfilled my heart's desire to serve?

I wanted to serve women who had been robbed of a beautiful experience in welcoming their child into this world. Women who were told that their bodies didn't work, that they couldn't birth the babies they had grown, or that they would never be able to have a natural birth. I wanted to help them take back their power and to speak into them, helping them overcome those past experiences by showing them that none of that was true. To help them believe in how they were created and how strong they truly are. Martha's questions drew out of me more than I could have ever imagined, and I was moved to action. I started my group where I could serve my people and started my custom website. This was just the beginning of me branding myself.

I didn't mention any of this to my husband. He was working pipeline, which meant that he had been gone for two to three weeks at a time with a twenty-four-hour turnaround on the weekends he came home. This lasted for almost two years. It was hard on all of us, and he didn't like missing out on our kids growing up. So he quit his job, and we took about six weeks to do some traveling and visit family. It was marvelous, except my dream was again pushed aside.

I felt like a liar, and to be honest, my stomach got upset every time I thought about talking to him about HBR and what I had started working on the few months before he was home for good. I was scared to tell him; I mean, this wasn't the first time that I had invested into some business training or worked with a coach. See, I had been going to business seminars for years, and although what I learned had changed our lives in many ways, my network marketing/MLM business was still not making us any money. On top of that, I had asked him earlier that year about working with another coach under a six-month contract, and he shot it down since I couldn't sell him on what it was she could actually help me with.

Telling him about HBR and my new vision for serving women on their journeys through pregnancy and childbirth put me in the puke zone. At that point, it was just my vision, and there was a ton of work to still be done. How could I get him to see and understand where I believed this could go? And yet, I felt bad that I wasn't working on my dream; I wasn't showing up for my people or providing any value in the group I had created with so much excitement.

So from September through to December, I didn't mention HBR or Martha, but the burning in my soul to get back to it was growing stronger with each day that passed. I was frustrated with myself for not doing something about it.

Then, at the beginning of January, we went out for date night, and I knew I couldn't stay quiet any longer. I needed time to focus on building this out and to see where it would lead to! It was gnawing at me, and I knew the nudge was really from God. I was seeing plenty of signs—from people reaching out to me about a post I had done, my group growing to over one hundred people overnight, and my inability to stop thinking about it. God had set me on this path with the purpose to serve women when He opened my eyes and gave me a supernatural belief that nobody could shake in the creation of my body to birth life.

So that night, I told Jonathan about HBR, the vision it had given me, and what I had already learned and implemented in July and August. As proof, I even showed him all the forms that I had printed and filled out to dig deep into who and how I would serve. Now that he was home every night, I felt that it was the perfect opportunity to set time aside for me to work on this vision. When he didn't answer and we kind of left the conversation hanging, I gave him time to process, and then I gave him options on what hours would fit our family evenings best. In the end, I got one hour a night four days a week where I could focus on my dream vision, and I was so excited to jump back in.

I'm not going to lie, in the beginning, he often didn't take my work hours seriously, and it got a little frustrating to me. Then, I started blogging weekly, connecting with more people, and was even scheduling interviews in the group I had created. He started to see a change in me and how I was talking. He saw the true excitement that was shining in me when I talked about what I was working on each week.

Today, I have been working on this for around eight months, and on top of consistently blogging and serving my group, I have launched coaching services, just finished a certification course to offer placenta preparation services, and I will be a published author twice by the end of the year. As I continue to grow and learn new concepts, I continue to see more and more opportunities to serve from my heart that can also become additional income streams for our family.

The biggest change for me is that my husband now regularly talks about how I will be making money beyond what we can imagine now. He is telling people that I am a coach building my own business and has even mentioned quitting his job to allow me more time to focus and continue growing. That is the biggest compliment I could ever get from him -- his belief, and his support. His confidence in me and belief in what I am creating means so much to me, and it propels me forward.

ABOUT AMANDA

Amanda Ignot is a wife, mother, empowered birther, entrepreneur, and natural birth coach. She currently lives in Columbia, Missouri with her husband and four children. She loves to educate and empower women to navigate their care and advocate for themselves throughout their pregnancy and child-birth journeys giving them back their power to envision the birth they truly are capable of. She is certified in placenta preparation and is beginning her studies to become a Doula/Birth Keeper. Her journey to motherhood was not an easy one, and yet she overcame the hard times, kept going, and had beautiful experiences along the way. Today you may find her traveling across the country, with her four children in tow, to attend the birth of a friend or accomplish her goals. Life is the adventure you make it to be.

Connect with Amanda at Findingamanda.com

27

KEILAH'S STORY

Everyone knows that person that sees something and says, "I could make that and sell it," right? That is me! But ... I rarely followed through. If I did get as far as doing the thing, then I didn't market it. If I did get far enough to market it, it fell flat because I never had any confidence in myself to show others I could provide value to them. I have tried so many things, but the only business I had any success with was a bread baking business. For my own health reasons, I learned how to take organic grains (I used twelve of them), grind them into flour, learned why grain should be sprouted (found an easier way), then made the most amazing bread! I still couldn't sell it!

Success came only by hubby selling it, and I hated the way he did it. He has zero issue with self-confidence, so he was like a circus barker when we showed up to the farmers markets. It got so that we would work different markets, so I didn't have to hear him. Was the problem him? Absolutely not—it was me! By the time we stopped that business, we had nine varieties of bread, and it took us two full days to bake for the one day of markets. Even that "success" was not enough money to support anyone, so the business was not sustainable. That business was put on hold, so I could be at my mom's side the last year of her life.

That was all happening as my babies were leaving the nest. After homeschooling them, off to college they went. My youngest was over a thousand miles away. People that know me say, "You are so successful; you have amazing kids." They are right; my kids are amazing, but my lack of confidence led me to believe that my kids were amazing, in spite of me. Both of them went to college on full scholarships, graduated, and are either in grad school or have finished grad school. They are amazing humans and are ready to serve the world. Momma is super proud of both of you!

You might be asking yourself, did some trauma happen to affect your confidence? No, but as one of five daughters of a very strong woman (and each of them are each very strong in their own right), I was a peace maker. I put the needs of others before my own, which you might be thinking is a good thing. You would be right, but when you spend your life putting everyone else first, then you are putting yourself last—always! When you are the last person you serve, you carry a lot, and I mean A LOT, of stress. You even get to the point where you believe you don't have permission to feel your emotions or dream your dreams. This has been the way I lived my life.

Thoughts from my head – "Don't call your sister (or a friend); if she needs help or wants to see you, she will reach out to you," or, "Don't speak up or stand out – you will be judged because you know you are not worth leading anyone."

To be brutally honest, there were times in my life that I believed those around me would be better off without me in their life, and I considered choosing to leave this world.

As I am sure you can tell, my life was a roller coaster of emotions. Most of the time, I didn't even allow myself to actually feel them. Do you know what your body does when you don't allow the emotions to be expressed? It buries them, it hides them, and it creates a bubble around that hiding spot. Not to get too weird on you, because this actually isn't weird, there are many scientific studies around this. When you have that bubble and don't deal/heal those emotions, it creates places in the body where your natural electricity can't move around that bubble. Then, that lack of flow can turn into many dis-ease states.

For the last twenty-plus years, I have been on a journey to wholeness. I have learned so many things over that time. I have learned how to eat to live instead of living to eat (food was my drug of choice). I have learned about all the toxic stuff in our food, in our water, in our air, in our clothes, in our furniture, and on and on. I love teaching people about these things because they then get to live a healthier life and teach their families to live a healthier life. For a while, I thought this was how I was supposed to serve the world.

A few years ago, as I was still struggling with my health, I was introduced to essential oils. Being raised on a farm, I knew about growing things in a way that benefits the plants and the earth. I knew this would be super important with concentrated things like essential oils, so I was careful with the ones I used. What I didn't realize was the most toxic thing in my life were my emotions. I was drawn to the oils that helped to calm my anxiety (that I didn't even realize I had until I had been using EOs for about six months). I was surviving in a daze. Having that tool led me back to my entrepreneur's heart, so I started working a business that allowed me to help others with all the toxicity in modern life.

Problem—again! Back to my lack of self-confidence, and marketing was a real struggle. That led me to following a bunch of trainers, buying training package after training package, all with little to no success. Honestly, some of the programs and trainers were crap, some were not. Again, the problem was me! I felt like quitting, and I sort of did at times. I would take a step back and then see another training and try again. The journey was not easy, but ultimately, even though I thought I quit a bunch of times, the fact that I am even writing this proves I didn't really quit.

In this mess, I was introduced to yet another trainer, Martha Krejci – what a fireball she is! I have always been attracted to strong women leaders. So, of course, I bought the course. And the next one she came out with and then ... the big one. Then, what did I do? Why, of course, I made tons and tons of money! That was what you expected to read, right?

Nope, I didn't because you know where Martha starts in her training? Get your mind in the right place, or you won't go anywhere! (She says it with so much love.) I knew she was right, but I had done so much work there that I thought I didn't need to do more, so I sat. I sat in my hard-headed mindset, and I sat in my hard-hearted emotions. But I kept listening and kept listening, knowing full well that I was not going to put my dreams down, now that I knew I had dreams. I believe the turning point for me was getting into a small group with other members of Martha's group as well as a new business opportunity that allows me to help so many more people all over the world. The small group helped this introvert with no self-confidence feel heard. I want to mention right here that the reason I didn't feel heard is, again, me! It is super hard for anyone to hear you when you don't speak. I didn't speak.

Let's talk for half a second about that new opportunity I

mentioned. It works with energy in the body, which is actually emotions! It is like maybe God had a plan or something. This opportunity opened up to me while the whole universe was closed down. Helping women (my heart is for that momma that is still in the daze and doesn't know she can dream of more) deal with life and emotions through energy just makes my heart sing. Now, I am using The Home-Based Revolution to learn to market this new opportunity, and my eyes have been opened to one tiny little thing Martha teaches (okay, there are several):

#1 - We all have something to share/teach others because we have all been through stuff. We are all valuable!

#2 - Having all your income coming from one source is not a good idea. Though excellent for my parents' generation, it is not the most intelligent strategy today.

#3 - I was playing at business – I am now serious. I am learning the skills of what it actually means to run a business.

Thank you, Martha!

I always thought I was attracted to strong female leaders because it what I always wanted to be but felt I could never be. Guess what the problem was? My emotions.

Now, I know I am who God created me to be – which is a strong, powerful woman!

ABOUT KEILAH

Keilah is a mid-life momma that has spent most of her life not knowing why she was even on the planet. She spent a large part of her life struggling with her health, diving deep into foods that bring LIFE into the body. That led to learning about quality foods (think GMO, toxic chemicals, etc) which led to learning the same about personal care products.

She came to the realization that her biggest problem was her mindset - she didn't know why she was here. Keilah's passion is helping stay at home moms realize that they don't have to be buried under the mess and chaos of their life. You (as a SAHM) need to find what lights your fire!

Keilah shares her knowledge of finding wellness, purpose & vision! Connect with her at https://linktr.ee/keilahsommer

ALSO BY MARTHA KREJCI

The Home-Based Revolution

Made in the USA
Monee, IL
14 November 2021